SANDRA,

The Israel Seder Haggadah

Ken Oritz

Thank you so much
for coming it was
great to see you.

Kenny

The Israel Seder Haggadah: Progressive Version
First Edition 2005
Daybreaks Gourmet
P.O. Box 1641
Fort Lee, NJ 07024

The author/publisher will be grateful for any information which will be of assistance in keeping future editions up to date. Readers may send correspondence to israelseder@earthlink.net. While reasonable care has been taken in the writing and development of this book, the author/publisher cannot accept liability for any consequences arising from the use thereof, or from the information contained therein.

Library of Congress control number 2005900122
ISBN 0-9764329-1-9

Printed in Toronto by
Webcom Limited
3480 Pharmacy Avenue
Toronto, Ontario
Canada M1W 2S7

Cover Artwork by Baruch Nachshon. Cover design and book design by Dayna Navaro daynan@earthlink.net

TABLE OF CONTENTS

The Israel Seder Haggadah

Ken Oritz

♦

"Even if you are dispersed to the uttermost parts
of the world, from there the L-rd your G-d will gather and fetch
you. From there the L-rd your G-d will bring
you into the land which your fathers possessed and you
shall possess it."

(Deuteronomy 30:5).

♦

DEDICATION

I dedicate this work in memory of my Tante Eva, who lit the fire of my soul, and in honor of Ariella and Leora, for whom I carry this torch.

I am deeply grateful to the people who have helped me with this manuscript: Jeanette Eichenwald, Rabbi Bob Carrole, Francyne Davis, Lori Wright–Weiss, Jennifer Di Piazza, Sara Esses–Eini, Jacob Etan Amir, Chef Cathy Kaufman, Dr. Elizabeth Scarlet, Lisa Magnes, David Ellisson, Nathan Kakshuri, Lonnie Ostrow and my dearest Sania. I am grateful for the time you have taken to listen to my thoughts and share with me your wisdom. You have been most helpful to me in structuring this Seder. Your friendship, concern, and belief in the power of my dreams have carried me through to this day.

Special thanks to The Jewish Agency for Israel, which was most gracious in granting permission to use its educational resources. Special Thanks to Orly Ganor for helping to translate brachot. A special thanks to Dayna Navaro, Gail Naron-Chalew, Charles Patterson, and Randa Dubnick.

I thank my mother, who has been a wonderful support.

I am grateful to my father, with whom I once shared weekly debates about the politics of Israel. I am grateful to have watched how he loved the land so passionately that I could not help but share his love. I appreciate how he shared with me his thoughts about the future of the land. I see now how prophetic many of his ideas were. He was my shepherd. As Nachman of Bratzlav once said, "When the heart is full from song, and yearns toward the land of Israel, a great light is drawn out and continues on.... From the song of the grass is created the melody of the heart." I pray that one day all of our hearts will be full and the great light will be drawn from Jerusalem, and on that day may the melody that emanates bring us all eternal peace.

I thank G-d for the blessed land of Israel, which has given me strength in my darkest hours. Its existence defies all logic. Its beauty grows and flourishes each day amidst an ocean of opposition and hatred. Its light continually becomes brighter and its future more promising. I write this Seder with all my love for the Holy Land and pray that whoever partakes in it will look with favor upon the land and the people of Israel and send them blessings.

INTRODUCTION

The Passover Seder commemorates the Exodus of the Jewish people from Egypt and their first redemption. It celebrates freedom from bondage and the giving of the Torah. It is based on these verses from the Torah:

"And I will free you from the labors of the Egyptians, and I will deliver you from their bondage. I will redeem you with an outstretched arm and through extraordinary chastisements. And I will take you to be my people and I will be to you a G-d. And I will take you into the land I swore to give Abraham, Isaac and Jacob and give it to you for a possession."[1]

Each aspect of the Exodus from Egypt is symbolized by the foods we eat and the successive cups of wine we drink at the Passover Seder. The one cup of wine we do not drink is the cup of Elijah. This cup symbolizes the Redemption of the Jewish people and their return to the land of Israel.

Many believe the creation of the State of Israel to be the dawn of the Redemption. However, some believe that the creation of the State of Israel is not a miracle but a momentous event in Jewish History. For the first time in nearly 2000 years Jews now have a land and a government that they can call their own. Whatever belief you hold, it is clear that the birth of the State of Israel is an event worthy of celebration. If you believe that the re-birth of the State of Israel is the beginning of the redemptive process then you may see this Seder as one based on the cup of Elijah. If, on the other hand, you believe that the rebirth of the State of Israel is merely a momentous event in Jewish History, then you may choose to see this Seder as a way to celebrate this event through the use of an ancient Jewish custom of using food to learn, celebrate and remember events in Jewish History.

At the Passover Seder we eat symbolic foods and drink successive cups of wine in order to remember our ancestors' Exodus from

Egypt. So too with this Seder we eat symbolic foods and drink successive cups of wine to remember successive events and periods of time that brought us closer to the founding of the State of Israel.

PREPARING FOR THE SEDER

The Purpose of Making Blessings

Many blessings are recited throughout this Seder. Some thank G-d for the wine or food, while others thank G-d for the many miracles which helped the Jewish people throughout history. Each blessing helps us to remember, celebrate, and learn.

When we eat and drink, we are receiving sustenance and allowing the food's energies to pass through us. This way of experiencing food is one of the greatest miracles that G-d provides for us each day. However, drinking wine and eating food only become holy acts when we make a blessing and acknowledge their source. When we bless the food and drink, the food and the energies carried with it are synthesized within our soul. In that way our recounting of Jewish history is integrated into our collective experiences as a people.

Wine

Wine or grape juice is an important component of every Jewish celebration. On Shabbat (the Sabbath celebration from Friday evening to Saturday night) we make a blessing over the wine and drink to mark the beginning of each of the three traditional Shabbat meals. On Saturday night in the Havdalah ceremony, we drink wine to separate Shabbat from the rest of the week. Additionally, we begin each Jewish holiday meal with a full glass of wine.

When preparing for this Seder, try to use a variety of wines that are produced in each of the wine growing regions of Israel. Serve the wine in small glasses so that each participant will be able to fully appreciate the varietals served. If you cannot find wines from each of Israel's wine producing regions, then make sure that all the wines are Israeli in origin. Information on Israeli wines and the regions where they are produced are found in Appendix G.

Remember, it is equally acceptable to serve/use grape juice for participants who don't drink alcohol. You can also purchase a variety of
Israeli juices and fruit nectars. Spring and Mitzli are bottled Israeli
fruit juices which are widely available in American markets.

The Seder Plate

Either have one large loaf of challah for the group or a small roll for
each participant.

Challah Bread

The challah that we eat at the Seder symbolizes the manna that,
according to the Torah, G-d sent to the Jewish people each morning
while they were wandering in the Sinai after fleeing Egypt. The manna
fed the Jewish people and was a sign that G-d was watching over
them.[2]

We eat challah at this Seder because it symbolizes the way in which G-
d continues to watch over the Jewish people throughout history and,
more specifically, how G-d helped the Jewish people reestablish the
State of Israel.

There is one final reason why we eat challah at this Seder. During the
time of both the First and Second Jewish Temples, which stood in
Jerusalem, two sets of six loaves of bread were placed on special racks
in the Temple. The holy, imminent presence of G-d (i.e., the
Shechinah) was said to dwell among these loaves of bread. So, too,
when we eat challah at this Seder, we invite the imminent presence of
G-d (the Shechinah) to join us and dwell among us at our table. [3]

Carob

Prepare a large dish with carob for the group, or give each participant
a piece of carob or carob chips.

The carob tree takes a very long time to bear fruit. According to the
Talmud, one who plants a carob tree may never be able to enjoy its

fruit. Therefore, the carob reminds us of those people who worked passionately to create the State of Israel, but never lived to see the fruits of their labor.

Root Vegetable

Use a root vegetable, such as a carrot, celery, potato, or parsnip.

The root vegetable is symbolic of how the Jewish people are rooted in the land of Israel

Edible Flower

Prepare an edible flower, or use floral scents to flavor a dish. Roses, orange blossoms, lavender, or orchids, or even foods flavored by the vanilla bean, are all acceptable.

The edible flower symbolizes the rebirth of the State of Israel and the way the land has blossomed and continues to blossom since its people have returned to it.

Stringed Vegetable

Cut a leek or scallion in half lengthwise and place it in boiling salted water for two minutes. Remove it and then place it in ice cold water. Take any vegetable such as a green bean or a peeled carrot and tie the leek or scallion skin loosely around it. Repeat to make one for each participant.

The tied vegetable is symbolic of the bonds that tie one Jew to another.

Fruit Grown in the Land of Israel

Prepare a plate of fruits grown in the land of Israel. Jaffa oranges, persimmons, or mangoes from the Sharon Valley, or even Carmel tomatoes, are all acceptable.

Seeds

Prepare a plate of sunflower, pumpkin, or squash seeds, or any other edible seed.

Seeds show possibility and potential. We hold the seeds in our hands to remind ourselves that each of us holds Israel's future in our hands.

The Seven Species

Prepare foods that incorporate the seven species of fruits and vegetables of the land of Israel: wheat, barley, grapes, figs, pomegranates, olives, and dates (or honey).

The Empty Chair

Reserve one empty chair at the table. Explain that this chair is for all of the Israeli soldiers who are missing in action and have not yet returned home. If the children are old enough to understand, you may also explain that this empty chair symbolizes the Israelis who were killed in terror attacks and were not able to join their families at the dinner table. The chair is left empty to symbolize the empty space in our hearts now that they are gone.

Causing the Seeds of Israel's Future to Grow

Prior to the Seder, reproduce Appendices L and M so that each participant has a copy at his or her place setting. Include a blank envelope with each photocopy. For the most updated lists and contact information, you may either log onto www.israelseder.com or simply email me at israelseder@earthlink.net.

The materials in these Appendices will be used throughout the Seder to encourage participants to think critically about how they can best help Israel. A list of organizations will be provided, and the participant will be asked to identify one organization, or one way he or she can best help. After the Seder the participant will fill out a short form and will send it to the organization of his or her choice. The form will tell the organization that he or she would like to help either by volunteering time, or by sending a monetary contribution to that organization. Each action we take on Israel's behalf allows it to be a stronger and more secure nation.

Preparing Your Children for the Seder

Explain to the children that you will be having a dinner to honor the State of Israel. Tell them that you need their help in preparing for the dinner. Ask them to draw a mizrach, which is a picture that will be hung on the eastern wall of your home to illustrate the direction of Jerusalem. If there are no children present or if children do not wish to draw a mizrach, you can then use an Israeli Flag to substitue for the mizrach. For other ways to incorporate your child or teenager into the Seder, see Appendices H, I, J, and K.

Appendices

To enhance the Seder experience, several readings and exercises are included in the Appendices for you to read or substitute as you wish. Some appendices offer you an alternative to what you are reading in the main text of the Seder while other appendices have exercises for children and teenagers. Still other Appendices offer information about Israel which is not part of the formal Seder, but is pertinent to it.

Like all Jewish customs old and new, this Seder is and always will be growing and changing. Your customs and preferences will help to shape and mold its future. Therefore, I invite you all to stay in touch with me and let me know how you use this Seder each year. Write me and let me know what readings you prefer and what things have you added. Your family customs may impact the future editions of this Seder. You may email me at: israelseder@earthlink.net.

ISRAEL SEDER

LEADER

Tonight we hold this Seder to remember the greatest miracle of our time. On May 14, 1948, on the 5th of Iyar in the year 5708, the State of Israel was reborn. Once again our people, who had been living in our land for the past 3,700 years, had reestablished our own government. Finally, our people who had been exiled to all corners of the earth had begun returning to the land of their ancestors.

Tonight we stand with every Jew around the world in unity and solidarity. We hold this Seder to proclaim to all the nations of the earth that we are one people with one faith and one heart and that we stand together with one voice. We call for the world to listen to its conscience and hear the plight of our people to live in peace, in our own Jewish country, in our ancestral homeland. We hold this Seder tonight to say to the world and to ourselves, AM YISRAEL CHAI (Long live the nation of Israel).

LEADER

For generations our people wandered in the Diaspora and prayed to return to the land of Israel and rebuild it. The rebirth of our nation marked the fulfillment of that long awaited dream.

We are fortunate to live in a time when our people can once again take their place among the nations. As we begin this celebration of our return to the land, we remember the first Jew who came to the land and made a covenant with G-d.

Abraham's Journey From Ur to Canaan

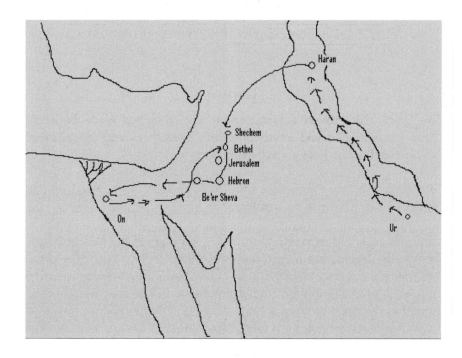

Abraham and Sara's Journey

Abraham and Sara journeyed to the land of Canaan in the seventeenth century B.C.E. They began their journey from their home in Ur, located in modern day Iraq, and continued north until they reached Haran. From there they journeyed onward to the land of Canaan where, according to Genesis (Chapter 13, Verse 15), G-d gave the land to Abraham and his descendents forever. However, due to famine, Abraham and Sara temporarily left the land and went to Egypt. They soon returned to Canaan to live out their lives in the land G-d gave to them.

כּוֹס רִישׁוֹן

THE FIRST CUP: THE CUP OF THE COVENANT

GROUP

We drink this cup in celebration of the covenant made between Abraham and G-d and in honor of the forefathers and foremothers who were the first Jews to settle the land.

We drink this cup in honor of the Torah we received at Sinai, which forever binds us to the land of Israel.

We drink this cup in memory of our ancestors, the Children of Israel, who, upon leaving the desert, settled the land and made it their own.

LEADER

Blessings

(All raise the cup of wine and recite)

Blessing on the Wine

Blessed are you Adonai, who has created the fruit of the vine.

The Shehechiyanu

Blessed are you Adonai, who has kept us alive, sustained us, and brought us to this season.

Ushpizin

(On the holiday of Sukkot, also known as the "Festival of Booths," it is customary to perform the Ushpizin service. This service welcomes the imminent presence of G-d, the Shechinah, as it accompanies the souls of major Jewish figures throughout history, while they visit the Sukkah to rejoice in the accomplishments of the Jewish people.[4]

This Ushpizin service invites the souls of major figures in Jewish history to join us and rejoice in the accomplishments of the Jewish people in returning to the land and reestablishing our government. For an alternate to this Ushpizin reading, see Appendix A; or for a Children's Experiential Ushpizin, see Appendix H.)

LEADER

To celebrate the rebirth of the State of Israel we invite great figures in Jewish history to join us and see the accomplishments of our people in rebuilding the land of Israel. We invite them to join us in our celebration.

GROUP

Be seated, exalted guests, be seated, be seated holy guests, be seated faithful guests, be seated in the imminent presence of G-d.[5] We are blessed to live in a time when our people have reestablished our government in the land of our ancestors. May our invited guests rejoice at the return of our people to the land, and may we rejoice in the return of a Jewish government for those who never left the land. May our guests bring with them the hope and prayers for peace and prosperity to the land.

The First Ushpizin

(To be read responsively)

We invite the exalted guest Abraham to whom G-d gave this land, as it is written: "For I give all the land that you see to you and your descendants forever. I will make your descendants as numerous as the stars in the heavens and give them all these lands so that the nations of the earth shall bless themselves by your offspring"[6]

We invite you to come and see how your children rebuilt the land of Israel in your honor.

We invite the exalted guests—Isaac, Jacob, Sara, Rebecca, and Leah—who were the first Jews to live in this Holy Land. We invite Rachel who weeps for her children's return to the land so they can find comfort there.

We invite you to come and see how your children rebuilt the land of Israel in your honor.

We invite the exalted guest, Moses, who led our ancestors out of Egypt, brought them to Mount Sinai where they received the Torah, and led them to the hills and outskirts of the promised land.

We invite you to come and see how your children rebuilt the land of Israel in your honor.

We invite the exalted guest Joshua, who led the children of Israel in settling the Holy Land and gave portions of it to each tribe.

We invite you to come and see how your children rebuilt the land of Israel in your honor.

We honor your spirit through our connection to the land of Israel.

The Sheva Minim or the Seven Species

(Pass the Seven Species around the table)

LEADER

After settling the land of Israel, our ancestors were rewarded with the fruits of the land.

The Torah designated seven forms of produce as the signature produce of the land of Israel:

"A land of wheat, barley and vines and figs and pomegranates, a land of oil yielding olives and dates."[7]

We celebrate this Jewish homecoming to the land by eating its produce. As we eat these fruits, we are reminded that even though more than 3,000 years have passed, the heart of our people remains forever and unchangeably connected to the land of Israel.

(All participants point to the Seven Species)

These fruits, vegetables, and grains were cultivated in the land of Israel by our people since they first settled the land after returning from forty years of wandering in the Sinai wilderness.

GROUP

(Participants take each of the Seven Species, or a prepared food that incorporates each one of the Seven Species. Everyone recites the first blessing together. Then, each participant recites the appropriate blessing for the food items chosen.)

Blessing on Sheva Minim

Blessed are you, Adonai, who has adorned the land of our ancestors with the seven species of produce.

Blessing on Wheat and Barley

Blessed are you, Adonai, who creates various kinds of foods.

Blessing on Grapes or Wine Made from Grapes

Blessed are you, Adonai, who has created the fruit of the vine.

Blessing on Figs, Pomegranates, Olives, and Dates

Blessed are you, Adonai, who brings forth fruit from the tree.

The Kingdoms of David and Solomon: 1077 - 997 BCE

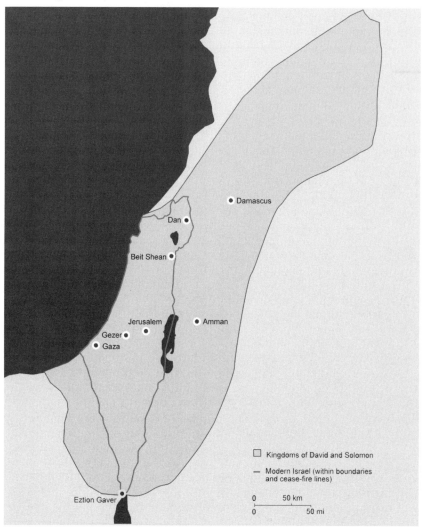

The Kingdoms of David and Solomon

"The Kingdoms of David and Solomon: 1077–997 BCE King David ruled Israel from 990 BCE to 968 BCE; and his son Solomon ruled after him until 928 BCE. David enlarged his kingdom and brought it to the peak of political and military power. Solomon "ruled over all the kingdoms west of the Euphrates River from Tiphsah to Gaza; he was at peace with all his neighbors" (I Kings, 4:24). Reproduced with permission by Reuven Koret, © Koret Communications Ltd. www.koret.com

כּוֹס שֵׁנִי

THE SECOND CUP:
THE CUP OF THE KINGDOM OF ISRAEL

(Refill and raise the cups of wine)

GROUP

We drink this cup in honor of the Judges who ruled Israel.

We drink this cup in honor of the Kingdoms of Israel and Judah.

We drink this cup in honor of the two Temples which once stood in Jerusalem.

LEADER

Blessing on the Wine

Blessed are you, Adonai, who has created the fruit of the vine.

(All drink the wine)

(See Appendix B for an optional reading for the Second Cup)

Second Ushpizin

We invite the exalted guests: Saul, David, Solomon, Josiah, Ezra, Nehemiah, Judah Maccabee, and Shimon Bar Kochba.

(All raise cups of wine)

PARTICIPANTS TAKE TURNS READING

We celebrate the Judges who governed our land for nearly 250 years.[8]

We invite King Saul, who was the first to be crowned King of Israel in Gilgal. [9]

We invite King David, who established the city of Jerusalem as the eternal capital of the Israel. [10]

We invite King Solomon, who built the first Temple in Jerusalem, where we brought sacrifices before G-d.[11]

We invite King Josiah, who protected the sanctity of the Temple by eliminating idolatry and rededicating the Temple.[12]

We honor the Jewish Kingdoms that flourished in our land for over 400 years.[13]

(Lowering the wine cups, each participant spills a drop of wine to symbolically remove a drop of happiness)

We remember with sadness when our Kingdoms were conquered by the Assyrians and Babylonians and our Temple was destroyed. We are saddened to remember our years of exile in Babylon.

(All raise wine cups)

We invite Ezra and Nehemiah, who led our people from their exile in Babylon and returned them to the Holy Land and rebuilt the Temple. [14]

(Lowering wine cups again, each participant spills a drop of wine to symbolically remove a drop of happiness)

We remember with sadness Antiochus IV, the Syrian Greek who desecrated our Temple and forbade us to do Mitzvot or learn Torah.

(All raise wine cups)

We invite Judah Maccabee, who resisted the Syrian Greek forces, reestablished our Temple, and freed us to practice Judaism openly and without fear.[15]

(Lowering the cups, each participant spills a drop of wine to symbolically remove a drop of happiness)

We weep to remember how the Romans razed Jerusalem, defiled our Temple, and killed many Jews while taking many others into slavery and captivity. [16]

(All raise wine cups)

We invite Shimon Bar Kochba, who led a resistance against the Roman Empire's hold over Judea. [17]

Jewish Communities in the Land of Israel (7th - 11th Centuries)

Jewish Communities in the Land of Israel (7th–11th Centuries)
"After the death of Emperor Julian II, in 363 CE, most of the Jewish settlements in the south were destroyed. The Jews remained mainly in the Galilee and in the larger cities." Reproduced with permission of Reuven Koret,© Koret Communications Ltd. www.koret.com

כּוֹס שְׁלִישִׁי

THE THIRD CUP: THE CUP OF HOPE

The Wanderings

(Refill and raise cup of wine)

GROUP

We drink this cup to remember how our people wandered the earth for almost 2000 years.

Blessing on the Wine

Blessed are you, Adonai, who has created the fruit of the vine.

(All drink the wine)

To the Jewish Communities Who Remained in our Land

(Participants take turns reciting paragraphs)

We honor the Jewish communities that remained in the land throughout the 2,000 years of our wandering. We honor those communities that flourished in Jerusalem and Tiberias and in Rafa, Gaza, Ashkelon, Jaffa, Caesarea, and Tzefat (Safed). [18]

We remember how we wandered the earth, as it was once prophesized: "You will become lost among the nations, and the land of your enemies will consume you" [19]

"Your sons and daughters will be given over to another people, and your eyes will see [this] and long for them all day long, but you will be powerless." [20]

We kept our faith and our connection to the land as we wandered and waited to return home.

For Additional Reading to Honor Rabbinic Legacy see Appendix C.

Eating the Root Vegetable

LEADER

We now eat a root vegetable (carrot, parsnip, celery, or potato) to symbolize that just as this vegetable was rooted in the earth, so too are the Jewish people rooted in the land of Israel.

GROUP

Blessing on our Connection to the Land of Israel

Blessed are you, Adonai, who has rooted the Jewish people in the land of Israel.

Blessing on the Root Vegetable

Blessed are you, Adonai, who creates the fruit of the earth.

Installation of the Mizrach

Children who were asked before the Seder to draw a picture to be hung on the eastern wall to signify the direction of the State of Israel are now invited to hang these pictures and point in the direction of Israel. If there are no children present, an Israeli flag may now be hung on the eastern wall of the room.

LEADER

(Recite while pointing to the Mizrach)

As we wandered, we kept our focus on the Holy Land, with Jerusalem centered in our hearts. We hung a picture on the eastern wall of our homes signifying the direction of Jerusalem, and we called this a "Mizrach." The Mizrach reminded us of the hope that our people would one day be able to return to the land of Israel and reestablish our State there. With that hope in mind, we faced Jerusalem each day as we prayed. Now that our people have returned to the land and reestablished our government there we continue to face Jerusalem and pray for its future.

With Eyes to Zion, We Strengthened Our Hope of Rebuilding the Land for Our People

(Each participant recites a paragraph in turn, with the group reciting responsively: "With eyes to Zion we strengthened our hope of rebuilding the land for our people.")

LEADER

In this reading we remember how our ancestors wandered from country to country after the destruction of the Second Temple in Jerusalem. While many Jews remained in the land, many others were scattered around the Mediterranean and fled to both Christian and later Muslim lands. This reading describes some of the Jewish experiences in both Muslim and Christian lands.

Wanderings in the Islamic World

We wandered to the Arabian Peninsula and sought to establish our-selves there, but Mohammed ordered the death of 900 Jews. [21]

GROUP

With eyes to Zion we strengthened our hope of rebuilding the land for our people.

The pact of Omar promised Jews and Christians that they could live peacefully in all Islamic countries, and so our people migrated to many areas in the Islamic Empire. However, in the seventh, eighth, twelfth, and fifteenth centuries, Muslims murdered entire cities of Jews in Morocco. In 1066, 5,000 Jews were put to death in Granada, Spain. Hundreds more were killed across North Africa in the eighteenth and nineteenth centuries. [22]

GROUP

With eyes to Zion we strengthened our hope to rebuild the land for our people.

Wanderings in the Christian World

We also migrated to the Christian lands. In the eleventh century, Crusaders murdered one third of the Jewish population in Northern France and Germany and committed massacres in Hungary, Ralisbon, and the Lorraine. [23]

GROUP

With eyes to Zion we strengthened our hope to rebuild the land for our people.

In the thirteenth and fourteenth centuries Crusaders pillaged another 260 Jewish communities across Europe. [24]

GROUP

With eyes to Zion we strengthened our hope to rebuild the land for our people.

In 1492 Queen Isabella of Spain decreed that all Jews in Spain must convert to Catholicism or face death. In the years to follow Jews in Spain and Portugal were executed for the sole crime of being Jewish. [25]

GROUP

With eyes to Zion we strengthened our hope to rebuild the land for our people.

In the seventeenth century 100,000 Jews were murdered in 300 communities throughout Russia. [26]

GROUP

With eyes to Zion we strengthened our hope to rebuild the land for our people.

The Holy Land Under Ottoman Rule

The Holy Land Under Ottoman Rule

Since the destruction of the Second Jewish Commonwealth by the Romans, a series of foreign empires conquered and then occupied the land. Such conquerors included; the Byzantines, the Arab Muslim Empire, the Seljuk Empire, the Crusaders, the Mamelukes, and finally the Ottoman Turks, who ruled the land from the year 1516 to 1917. *Reproduced with permission from the collection by Dr Motti Friedman, The Pedagogic Center, The Department for Jewish Zionist Education, The Jewish Agency for Israel (C), http://www.jafi.org.il/education/100/maps/ottoman.html*

כּוֹס רְבִיעִי

THE FOURTH CUP: THE CUP OF REBIRTH

The Rebirth of the Land and the Homecoming of Its Children

(Refill and raise wine cups)

GROUP

We drink this cup to honor the rebirth of the land as the Jews who were natives to the land of Israel welcomed the first homecoming of their exiled brothers and sisters.

Blessing on the Wine

Blessed are you, Adonai, who has created the fruit of the vine.

(All drink the wine)

LEADER

In 1882 fewer than 250,000 Arabs lived in the land, before the first wave of Jewish settlers arrived to join their people. Mark Twain wrote about his visit to the Holy Land during this period, describing it as "a desolate country whose soil is rich enough, but is given over wholly to weeds, a silent mournful expanse...a desolation is here that not even imagination can grace with the pomp of life and action... We never saw a human being on the whole route... There was hardly a tree or shrub anywhere. Even the olive and cactus, those fast friends of the worthless soil, had almost deserted the country." [27]

In the darkness of the Diaspora the dream of rebuilding our homeland became ever more pressing. In 1897 Jews came to Basel Switzerland for the first Zionist Congress from all parts of Europe and Russia. Jews who were observant and Jews who were secular worked together to make the idea of Israel possible under the leadership of Theodor Herzl. [28]

To learn more about the great Zionist thinkers of the nineteenth and twentieth centuries, see "The Timeless Zionist Congress" in Appendix H.

Eating the Carob

PARTICIPANT

Rabbi Yochanan said: "One day, Honi the Circle Maker was walking on the road, and he saw a man planting a carob tree. He asked him, 'How long will it take this tree to bear fruit?' The man replied, 'Seventy years.' He asked, 'Are you quite sure you will live another seventy years to eat its fruit? The man replied, 'I myself found fully grown carob trees in the world; as my forebears planted for me, so am I planting for my children.'"[29]

LEADER

We eat the carob to remember the many Jews who came before us and sacrificed to build a Jewish State in the land of Israel but did not live to see its rebirth.

Blessing on the Legacy of Zionism

Blessed are you, Adonai, who has enabled our ancestors to pass on the torch of Zionism throughout the generations.

Blessing on Carob Fruit

Blessed are you, Adonai, who has created the fruit of tree.

Blessing on Carob Chips

Blessed are you, Adonai, who creates various foods.

(All eat the carob)

We Will Not Forget: A Responsive Reading

PARTICIPANT

In 1881-83, hundreds of Russian mobs murdered thousands of their fellow Jewish citizens in widespread pogroms. The Russian government supported the regular murder of Jews.[30]

GROUP

We will not forget.

PARTICIPANT

During the Holocaust the world was silent while six million Jews were murdered. Even America and Canada locked its doors to those trying to escape Hitler. [31]

GROUP

We will not forget.

PARTICIPANT

On the eve of the Holocaust Great Britain issued the "White Paper" to prevent Jews from entering British-mandated Palestine so that no Jews were allowed to enter the land when the need for safety was the greatest.[32]

GROUP

We will not forget.

PARTICIPANT

Yet amidst our frightful experiences in the Diaspora, we were sustained by hope, and our resolve gave birth to a new song, the song of hope, "Hatikvah."

"The Hatikvah," (The Hope)
Israel's National Anthem

GROUP
(Led by the Children Present)

Hatikvah   **Transliteration**   הַתִּקְוָה

Kol od balevav penima   כָּל עוֹד בַּלֵּבָב פְּנִימָה
nefesh yehudi homia,   נֶפֶשׁ יְהוּדִי הוֹמִיָּה,
oulfa'atey mizrakh kadima   וּלְפַאֲתֵי מִיזְרָח קָדִימָה
ayn leTzion tzofia.   עַיִן לְצִיּוֹן צוֹפִיָּה–

Od lo avda tikvatenou,   עוֹד לֹא אָבְדָה תִּקְוָתֵנוּ,
hatikva ba shnot alpayim,   הַתִּקְוָה בַּת שְׁנוֹת אַלְפַּיִם,
lihiot am khofshi be'artzenu   לִהְיוֹת עַם חָפְשִׁי בְּאַרְצֵינוּ
Eretz Tzion Vrushalayim   אֶרֶץ צִיּוֹן וִירוּשָׁלַיִם.

Translation of the Hatikva

As long as deep in the heart,
The soul of a Jew yearns,
And towards the East,
An eye looks to Zion. Our hope is not yet lost,
The hope of two thousand years,
To be a free people in our land,
The land of Zion and Jerusalem.[33]

LEADER

"Behold the guardian of Israel, he does not sleep nor slumber." [34]

Eating the Root Vegetable with the Strand of Scallion
(Each participant takes a strand of scallion or leek and ties it to a vegetable, such as a carrot or string bean.)

LEADER

We now eat a root vegetable tied to another vegetable to symbolize the bonds that tie one Jew to another. We celebrate this brotherhood and sisterhood of our people. We recognize that it has lasted throughout history and has been one of the main reasons for our survival. We realize that this bond, if nourished, will help us continually build flourishing Jewish communities.

GROUP
Blessing on the Tied Vegetable

Blessed are you, Adonai, who creates the fruit of the land.

(All eat the tied vegetable)

The British Mandate

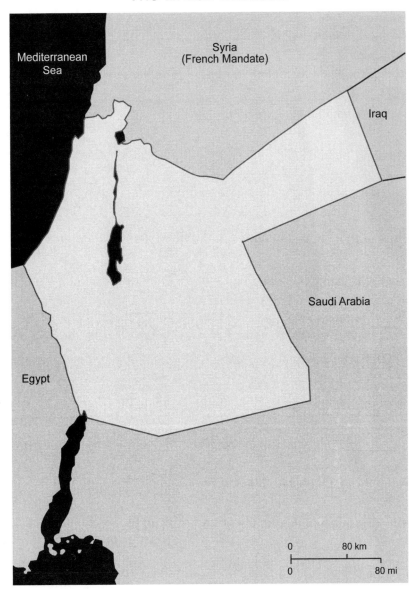

British Mandated Palestine
In 1920, the League of Nations gave Great Britain the mandate for the Land of Israel
and Transjordan with the purpose of preparing it for a "National Jewish Homeland."
There were no territorial restrictions given to the Jews settling this area east or west of
the Jordan River. *Reproduced with permission by Reuven Koret, © Koret Communications
Ltd.www.koret.com*

The British Division of Palestine

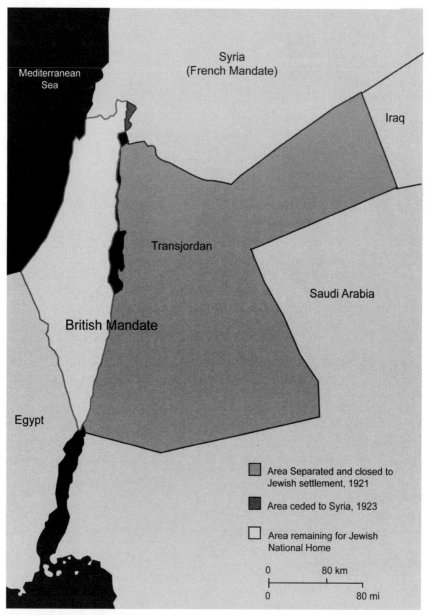

The British Division of Palestine

In 1922, the British decided independently to decrease the size of the future Jewish National Homeland to only 22% of its former size and permitted Jewish settlement only west of the Jordan River. East of the Jordan River became known as "TransJordan" and the British appointed a Hashemite Ruler, Abdullah, who was expelled from the Arabian Pennisula. *Reproduced with permission by Reuven Koret, © Koret Communications Ltd. www.koret.com*

1947 UN Partition Plan

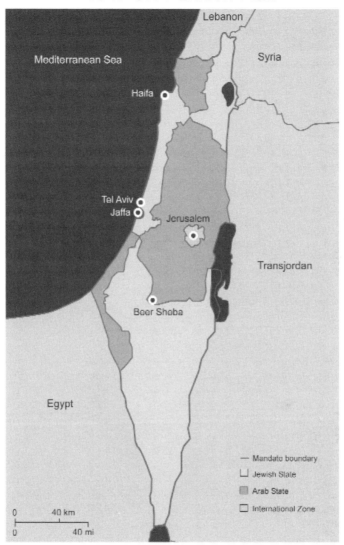

1947 UN Partition Plan

"In 1947, Great Britain relinquished to the UN the power to make decisions relating to the status of the Land of Israel. The General Assembly appointed a special committee that collected evidence and decided unanimously that Israel should be granted independence.

Most of the committee members favored partitioning the land into two states, a Jewish state and an Arab state, with Jerusalem under international supervision. On November 29, 1947, the UN General Assembly accepted the partition resolution, 33 to 13." *Reproduced with permission by Reuven Koret, © Koret Communications Ltd. www.koret.com*

1949–1967 Armistice Lines

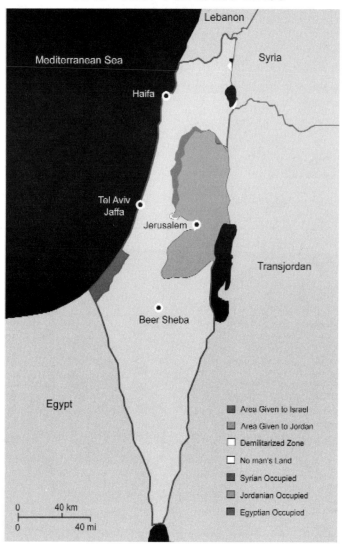

1949–1967 Armistice Lines
In the spring and summer of 1949, agreements were signed between Israel and its neighbors establishing Israel's armistice lines. To some extent, these lines overlapped the borderline of Palestine during the British mandate or were close to it, with the exception of the Judea and Samaria region, and the surrounding area of the Gaza strip. These lines were drawn up on the assumption that they would be temporary, and would be replaced within a few years by permanent borders. *Reproduced with permission by Reuven Koret,* © *Koret Communications Ltd. www.koret.com*

כּוֹס חֲמִישִׁי

FIFTH CUP OF WINE:
ESTABLISHMENT OF THE STATE OF ISRAEL
AND THE INGATHERING OF THE EXILED

(Refill and raise wine cups)

LEADER

We drink this cup to honor the birth of the State of Israel and to celebrate the many Jews who have returned to the home of their ancestors.

Blessing on the Wine

Blessed are you, Adonai, who has created the fruit of the vine.

Blessing on the Establishment of the State of Israel

Blessed are you, Adonai, who caused the great miracle of our time, the creation of the State of Israel, and the ingathering of the exiled.

(All drink the wine)

LEADER

As it was prophesized, "Fear not for I am with you: I will bring your seed from the East and gather you from the West. I shall say to the North, give up, and to the South, do not hold back, bring my sons from far and my daughters from the end of the earth" [35]

Celebrating the Ingathering of the Exiled

GROUP

To the East
From where have you come, my brother?

PARTICIPANT

I have saddled a donkey and crossed the mountains of Iran and Iraq, I have traveled from as far as China, India, and Afghanistan, and as near as Syria and Lebanon to return home and join my people.

GROUP

To the West
From where have you come, my sister?

PARTICIPANT

From Morocco I have swept across the deserts of North Africa and walked across Algeria, Tunisia, Libya, and Egypt. I have set sail by boat and by plane from Italy, France, Spain, England, Argentina, Colombia, Bolivia, Peru, Mexico, Cuba, Canada, and the United States to return home.

GROUP

To the North
From where have you come, my brother?

PARTICIPANT

I have escaped Polish pogroms where thousands of Jews from my village were killed before my eyes. I have fled Hitler from Germany, France, Hungary, Austria, Romania, and Russia. I have been rescued by the Jewish partisans who resisted the Nazis and brought me to this blessed land where I can be free.

GROUP

To the South

From where have you come, my sister?

PARTICIPANT

I have been lifted onto the wings of eagles and flown over the deserts of Sudan and Saudi Arabia and brought home from Yemen and Ethiopia.

GROUP

From the Land of Israel

From where have you come, my brothers and sisters?

PARTICIPANT

I have never left this sacred land. For I have lived in Jerusalem, Hebron, Tiberias, Gaza, Rafa, Ashkelon, and Tzefat for 3,700 years and now that you, my brothers and sisters, have returned home, together we will cause this land to flourish.

LEADER

As it was prophesized, "And it shall come to pass in that day that a great shofar shall be blown, and they shall come that were lost in the land of Assyria, and they that were dispersed in the land of Egypt, and they shall worship the L-rd in the holy mountain of Jerusalem"[36]

Blessing on the Ingathering of the Exiles

Blessed are you, Adonai, who continually enables the Jewish people to return to the land of their ancestors.

כּוֹס שִׁישִׁי

THE SIXTH CUP:
THE CUP OF THE FLOURISHING LAND

(Refill and raise wine cups)

LEADER

We drink this cup to honor the many ways the land has blossomed since its people have returned to it.

Blessing on the Wine

Blessed are you, Adonai, who has created the fruit of the vine.

(All drink the wine)

GROUP

As it was prophesized, "And the desert shall rejoice and blossom as a rose." [37]

As it was prophesized, "The earth will manifest fertility, yielding an over-abundance of every kind of produce, and trees growing ripe fruits every day. Zion's wilderness will be made to be like Eden, and her desert like a garden of G-d." [38]

Eating an Edible Flower

(During this part of the Seder participants make a blessing on an edible flower. Then they eat the edible flower to symbolize Israel's thriving agriculture. Lavender, roses, orange blossoms, or any other edible flower is acceptable. If none are available, then foods with floral scents or flavors (including vanilla) can also be eaten).

Blessing for the Land of Israel

Blessed are you, Adonai, who has caused the land of Israel to flourish when its people return to it.

Blessing on an Edible Flower

Blessed are you, Adonai, who creates flowers from the earth.

Blessing for a Food Made from a Flower Product (such as rose water or lily water)

Blessed are you, Adonai, who creates various kinds of foods.

(All eat the flower or flower product)

Eretz, Eretz:

A Responsive Reading Recited Alternatively by Leader and Group

GROUP

Eretz, Eretz, Eretz: How have you blossomed?

LEADER

We caused cities to arise from the sand and built the ports of Eilat and Haifa.

GROUP

Eretz, Eretz, Eretz: How have you blossomed?

LEADER

We built roads that connected our cities and installed plumbing and electricity for ourselves and our Arab neighbors.

GROUP

Eretz, Eretz, Eretz: How have you blossomed?

LEADER

We established Kibbutzim and Moshavim and caused the Negev desert in the south to bloom in a rainbow's spectrum of flowers.

GROUP

Eretz, Eretz, Eretz: How have you blossomed?

LEADER

We caused the Galilee in the north to produce large yields of luscious produce. Where there were once barren fields, there are now orchards and vegetable groves and fruit trees.

In every corner, you the land of Israel have blossomed with flowers and plants and all types of produce. To celebrate your growth we look to the heavens and thank G-d for the warm Israeli sun, and the rain and dew that made it possible to cultivate the land. We look to the earth and thank G-d for a soil that is rich in minerals and nutrients. We look to the land and find the many temperate zones that comprise such a small country. We look to the produce of the land as a symbol of all that we have accomplished with the help of G-d.

Blessing on Israeli Produce

(Each participant takes one serving of fruit or vegetable grown in the land of Israel, holds it up, and makes the appropriate blessing.)

Blessed are you, Adonai, who has infused the produce of the land of Israel with a unique and delicious taste.

Blessing on the Fruit

Blessed are you, Adonai, who has created the fruit of the tree.

(All eat the Israeli produce)

Hand Washing

(Before beginning the Seder meal, it is customary for each participant to wash his or her hands and then make a blessing over the challah.)

The process of eating food in Judaism is seen as a way to synthesize the spiritual properties of the food with the spiritual energies of our soul. Therefore, our hands are viewed as receptacles of this energy, and because of this they must be cleansed both literally and spiritually.

The Traditional Method of Spiritual Hand Washing

Before the meal participants wash their hands by taking a cup and filling it with water and pouring water on each hand, switching back and forth between the two hands. After two cups of water are spilled on each hand, the following blessing is recited.

Blessing for Hand Washing

Blessed are you, Adonai, who makes us holy by sanctifying our meal with the mitzvah of washing of our hands.

LEADER

Hamotzi: Blessing on the Challah

(Before making the blessing over bread, each participant either holds a challah roll, or places a hand on the large challah and recites the following blessing.)

Blessed are you, Adonai, for bringing forth bread from the earth.

Meal

(The meal should now be served)

Birkat HaMazon: Grace After The Meal

(After the meal is over, the grace is recited. Upon its conclusion, the Seder continues.)

Leader
My friends let us make the blessing.

Group
May G-d's name be blessed from now and forever.

Leader
May G-d's name be blessed from now and forever.
In the presence and with the consent of all those present, let us bless G-d for the food we have eaten.

Group
Blessed is G-d whose food we have eaten and through whose goodness we live.

Leader
Blessed is G-d whose food we have eaten and through whose goodness we live.
May G-d be blessed and may G-d's name be blessed.

All Present
You are blessed L-rd who provides sustenance for the entire universe in goodness, kindness and mercy. You provide bread for all living beings through your everlasting loving kindness.

Because of your kindness we have never lacked for food and we will never lack for it. Because of your Magnificent name, and because you are G-d who feeds all, takes care of all and supplies food for all you have brought into being. You are blessed G-d who supplies food for all.

We thank You G-d, for the heritage of the good, desirable and spacious land of Israel, you graciously gave to our ancestors, and for rescuing us from slavery and bondage, and for your Torah, which you imparted to us and for the life of grace and mercy which you have bestowed upon us.

It is written "And you shall eat and be satisfied and bless the L-rd your G-d for the good land he gave you.

You are blessed G-d for the good land and the food.

May the beautiful and holy city of Jerusalem be built up speedily in our lifetimes. Blessed are you Adonai who builds Jerusalem in honor and peace. Amen.

LEADER
May the All Merciful sustain us and the State of Israel in honor and peace.

GROUP
Amen.

LEADER
May the All Merciful bless all assembled at this (these) table(s).

GROUP
Amen.

LEADER
May the All Merciful bless the State of Israel and protect her.

GROUP
Amen.

LEADER
May the All Merciful help us to guide our actions and deeds to create a just and peaceful world.

GROUP
Amen.

ALL PRESENT
May the one who makes peace in high places, make peace for us and for all of Israel.

LEADER

(Refill and raise cups of wine)

In honor of Jerusalem

(Refill and raise cups of wine)

Leader

We thank G-d for returning us to Jerusalem and allowing us to take part in its rebuilding.

(Individual Participants take turns reading responsively with the Group)

Participant

In 1967 the first Jewish army since the time of Bar Kochba entered the walls of Jerusalem and reunited our city, the eternal capital of our people. We remember the verse from the Talmud: "Ten portions of beauty descended from heaven to the world. Jerusalem received nine of them and the rest of the world one."[39]

GROUP

We seek to rebuild Jerusalem in all of its glory. "May the L-rd bless you from Zion. And may you see Jerusalem in its goodness all the days of your life." [40]

Israel and the Six Day War

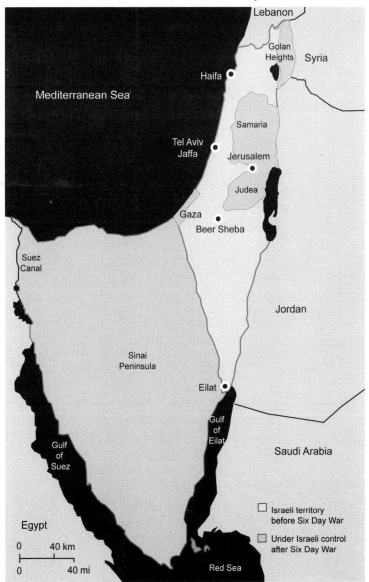

Israel and the Six Day War

With Arab armies mounted and poised to strike, Israel launched a pre-emptive attack on the massive Egyptian forces aimed at her. At the same time Israel issued an appeal to Jordan to stay out of the war. Jordan refused and opened fire on west Jerusalem and the Tel Aviv area which forced Israel to counter attack. The six days of fierce fighting ended with Israel capturing east Jerusalem, the Sinai Desert, the Gaza Strip, the Golan Heights, the areas of Judea and Samaria (also known as the West Bank). Cited from *The Jewish Agency for Israel website* ©, *http://www.jafi.org.il/education/100/maps Maps Reproduced with permission by Reuven Koret, © Koret Communications Ltd. www.koret.com*

Jerusalem and the Six Day War (1967)

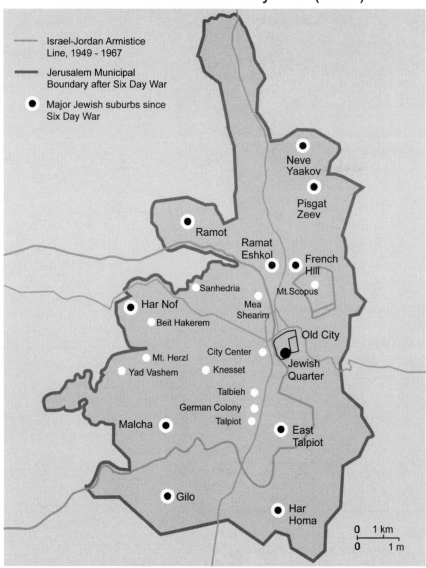

Legend:
- Israel-Jordan Armistice Line, 1949 - 1967
- Jerusalem Municipal Boundary after Six Day War
- ● Major Jewish suburbs since Six Day War

Neve Yaakov

Pisgat Zeev

Ramot

Ramat Eshkol

French Hill

Sanhedria

Mt.Scopus

Har Nof

Mea Shearim

Beit Hakerem

Old City

Mt. Herzl

City Center

Jewish Quarter

Yad Vashem

Knesset

Talbieh

German Colony

Talpiot

Malcha

East Talpiot

Gilo

Har Homa

0   1 km
0   1 m

Jerusalem and the Six Day War (1967)
A few days after the end of the Six-Day War, on June 27th, 1967 The Israeli Parliament passed a law that Israeli administration and jurisdiction apply to all the territory of Jerusalem acquired in the war. The following day, the Jerusalem municipal boundaries were extended to include eastern Jerusalem, as well as, Atarot and Neve Yaakov in the north and Gilo in the south. *Maps Reproduced with permission by Reuven Koret, © Koret Communications Ltd. www.koret.com*

Modern Israel (within boundaries and cease-fire lines)

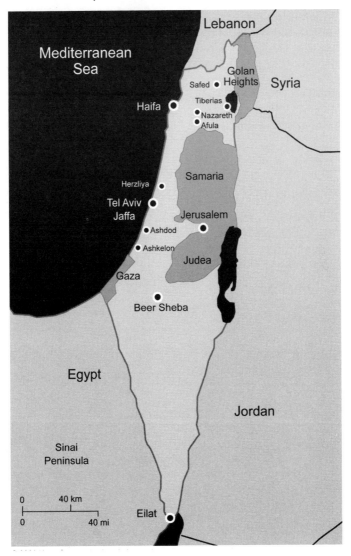

Modern Israel (within boundaries and cease-fire lines)
"Israel stands at the crossroads of Europe, Asia and Africa. Geographically, it belongs to the Asian continent. Its western border is the Mediterranean Sea. To the north it is bound by Lebanon and Syria, to the east by Jordan and to the south by the Red Sea and Egypt. Long and narrow in shape, Israel is about 290 miles (470 km.) long and 85 miles (135 km.) across at its widest point. Its total area is 22,145 sq km, of which 21,671 sq km is land area." *Reproduced with permission by Reuven Koret,"* © *Koret Communications Ltd. www.koret.com*

כּוֹס שְׁבִיעִי

THE SEVENTH CUP: THE CUP OF EXISTENCE

(Refill and raise cups of wine)

LEADER

This is the cup of the present time. We drink it to remind ourselves that the future existence of the State of Israel depends on each of us.

Blessing on the Wine

Blessed are you, Adonai, who has created the fruit of the vine.

(All drink the wine)

PARTICIPANT

(Participants take turns reading aloud)

Each of the previous cups celebrated the miracles and wonders that G-d performed for us in the past. We celebrated those who came before us and made history, reaffirming our connection to the land. This cup, however, is about our present place and time in history as Jews and as people connected emotionally, spiritually, and intellectually to the State of Israel.

PARTICIPANT

We know that the State of Israel provides a safe haven for Jews around the world who are subjected to anti-Semitism. We also know that the State of Israel provides a place where Jews can live among other Jews in a Jewish culture and Jewish society. Israel is a place where Jews can live out their own Jewish destiny without explanation or the awkwardness of living in a non-Jewish society.

PARTICIPANT

The existence of the Israel Defense Forces is the only way for Israel to protect its rights and its society. The Israeli Army defends the rights of Jews in Israel to practice Judaism freely and to live a Jewish life. This right allows all Jews around the world the comfort of knowing that they too can practice Judaism freely and can live a Jewish life. The Israeli Defense Forces defends Israel against those who seek its destruction. We pray for the continued strength of the Israeli Army to successfully defend our people, our society, and our culture.

Prayer for the Israel Defense Forces

GROUP

May G-d who blessed our ancestors—Abraham, Isaac, and Jacob, Sara, Rebecca, Rachel and Leah—bless the soldiers of the Israel Defense Forces and the security personnel who stand guard over the land of our ancestors—from the Lebanese border to the Egyptian wilderness, from the Mediterranean Sea to the edges of the desert, or wherever they might be on land, in the air, or at sea.

May G-d cause our enemies who attack us to suffer defeat at the hands of our troops. May G-d shield and protect them from any adversity or anguish, any ordeal or suffering, and send blessings and success to everything they do.[41]

(For an additional reading, see "Spilling Wine in Memory of Those Killed in Self-Defense," Appendix D)

The Empty Chair/The Un-Drunk Cup

LEADER

We leave one cup filled but not drunk, and we leave one chair empty to symbolize the Israeli soldiers whose place at the table is vacant since they have been killed in a terror attack. We also leave this chair empty to symbolize the many Jews who cannot join their families at the dinner table because they too were killed in a terror attack. We remember the Israeli soldiers who are still missing in action.

(See Appendix E for an Optional Prayer for Israeli Soldiers Missing in Action)

GROUP

As it is written in the Talmud, "The sword is worse than death, famine is harder than the sword, captivity is worst of all." [44]

Eating Seeds

(Each participant takes some edible seeds and passes them around the table. Pumpkin, squash, and sunflower seeds are all acceptable)

LEADER

The future of Israel is in our hands. What we do or don't do can affect whether Israel continues to exist. The actions we take today and tomorrow can have a direct impact on the lives of our fellow Jews who live in Israel. We have the opportunity to nurture the seeds of Zion. We have the chance to cultivate our love of Israel and watch that love help Israel grow.

For the sake of ourselves and our people we must support Israel. We must make sure that Israel's people are safe. We can affect U.S. policy on the Middle East. We have an opportunity to make a difference.

(For an additional reading, see "I Hold the Seeds to Israel's Future," Appendix F)

Before reciting the blessing over the seeds, review the list of organizations that support Israel (either use the list of Organizations that were handed out to you or use the list found in Appendix M) and think of a way you can become involved in lending support to Israel. Decide how you can best help this week, this month, this year. Decide how you can volunteer your time, your skills, and your energy, or simply send a generous donation to an organization that is in dire need of your help.

After the Seder has concluded, use the contact form provided to alert the organization you chose to let them know how you are available to help. In this way you will personally have a stake in the future of the Jewish people and the State of Israel.

Group

We now eat these seeds and reflect on the ways we can affect Israel's future. We now consider how we hold the lives of our fellow Jews in our hands. These seeds we hold are symbolic of the future of the State of Israel and the future potential of the Jewish people.

Blessing on the Opportunity to Advocate for the State of Israel

Blessed are you Adonai, who grants us the opportunity to help our brothers and sisters in the State of Israel by speaking out and advocating for them. Blessed are you G-d, who empowers us with the ability and will to strengthen and secure their future.

Blessing on the Seeds

*(As seeds are passed around the table, each participant takes
a small handful of them.)*

Blessed are you, L-rd our G-d, Master of the Universe, who creates the fruit of the earth.

(All eat the seeds)

Bracha Achrona

You are blessed Adonai for food and nourishment and for the vine and the fruit it bears, and for the produce and for the lovely, fine and spacious land which you graciously gave to our ancestors as a heritage to eat of its fruit and to be sated with its goodness. Have Mercy, our G-d, on Israel, Your people; on Jerusalem, Your city and on Zion the home of your glory. May you build up Jerusalem, the holy city, rapidly in our lifetimes. Bring us there so that we may rejoice in its rebuilding, eat of its fruit and be sated with its goodness. And there we will bless you in holiness and in purity.

For You G-d are good and you do good to all, and we thank you for the land and for the fruit of its vine. You are blessed Adonai, Sovereign of the world, creator of many kinds of life and their needs, for everything which You created to sustain all life. You are blessed, O' Eternal One. [43]

LEADER

We end the Israel Independence Day Seder with the words of the prophet Isaiah.

GROUP

(Recite responsively)

"For Jerusalem's sake I will not be still."

"For Jerusalem's sake I will not be still."

"And for Zion's sake I will not be silent."

"And for Zion's sake I will not be silent."

"Till her victory emerges resplendent."

"Till her victory emerges resplendent."

"And her triumph like a flaming torch."

"And her triumph like a flaming torch."[44]

L'Shana Ha Zot B'Yerushalayim

This year in Jerusalem

LEADER

This concludes our Seder. This year may we all celebrate an eternal peace in the land of Israel. May we all be there together in Jerusalem as it was in days of old.

APPENDIX A

THIS IS THE LAND OF OUR INHERITANCE

Participants take turns Reading Responsively

We honor the Land of Israel that was given to our ancestor Abraham by G-d, as it is written, "For I give all the land that you see to you and your descendants forever."[45]

We honor the Holy Land in which Isaac was the first Jew to live all the days of his life.

We honor the land where Jacob wrestled with an angel and won and for that was renamed Israel.[46]

We honor the land where the twelve sons of Jacob lived freely.

We honor the land that our people dreamt of for 400 years when they were enslaved in Egypt.[47]

We honor the land that our people dreamt of when they rose up from Egypt and broke free from their bondage.

We honor the land and our connection to it that was reaffirmed at Mount Sinai.

We honor the land that Moses gazed upon from east of the Jordan on Mount Nebo.[48]

We honor the land that the Children of Israel returned to under Joshua's leadership.[49]

We honor the land that G-d adorned with the Seven Species to welcome our ancestors when they came in from the wilderness.[50]

APPENDIX B

I HAVE HEARED THE LAND SPEAK

Participants Take Turns Reading Responsively

I have been to the land of my ancestors. I have seen the land that my people have loved, and I have heard it speak.

I have heard Jericho and Jerusalem speak of a time when the children of Israel conquered them under Joshua's leadership.[51]

I have heard Gaza speak of Samson, who grasped the pillars of a building which held those who sought his demise and caused the building to collapse.[52]

I have been to Beer Sheva, Hebron, and Jerusalem, and I have heard the land speak of the Judges who once ruled nobly there.[53]

In Ramah and Beth El I heard the land speak of a time when the people of Israel sang praises to Deborah for reopening their cities.[54]

Gilgal recalled the time when Saul was crowned King of Israel.[55]

The city of Bethlehem spoke of a small young man who herded sheep and played the harp. The hills of Jerusalem cheered when that little shepherd slew the great giant. Hebron rejoiced and sang when that man named David, was anointed King.[56]

I heard Mount Moriah whisper memories of King Solomon, who once built a great Temple on that very spot. [57]

The land wept as it told me of this Temple's destruction and the exile of its people to Babylon.[58]

The land rejoiced in memory of Ezra and Nechemiah, who brought back the exiled from Babylon and rebuilt the Temple.[59]

Mount Arbel remembered the Macabees who used its apex as a lookout point. The winds of the Galilee whispered the tale of a small Judean army that defended a massive onslaught of Syrian Greek forces who sought to end their observance mitzvoth and make them lose interest in learning Torah.[60]

The streets of Yavneh and Bnei Brak reveled in memory of the great schools of Torah that once flourished there. The voices of the great Rabbis of the Mishnah still echo through those streets.[61]

The shores of Caesarea and the walls of Jerusalem wept in memory of the destruction of the Second Temple and the exile of Jews from Jerusalem.[62]

The City of Betar echoed the commands of Bar Kochba as he led the last great Jewish rebellion. [63]

The land cried out in memory of its people who were sent away to restlessly wander the earth.

APPENDIX C

THE USHPIZIN OF THE SAGES

LEADER

As we remember 2,000 years of our wanderings, we honor the lineage of Rabbis who through their work and dedication passed down the light of the Torah and love of Zion from generation to generation. The light that was passed down from our forefathers and foremothers ensured that we as a people would one day return to the land and rebuild it. We remember our great sages who led us through the times we wandered the Diaspora. We honor their lives, and we acknowledge the gifts of their work. G-d gave the land of Israel to the Jewish people, but we have returned to it and redeemed it because our sages kept the spark of Judaism and love of Zion alive throughout our wanderings.

Gather around and be seated, holy guests; gather around and be seated, exalted guests. We invite our great sages and learned men of Torah who have built Jewish communities and fostered the hope of returning to the land while we wandered throughout the Diaspora. We invite these wise scholars to come and join us at the table as we rejoice in our people's return to the land.

[In this ceremony each participant holds an unlit candle. The first participant lights the candle, reciting the names of the sages; "Akiva and Bruria" and then passes the flame to the next participant, who recites the name of the next sage, and so on down the line. After reciting each name the lit candle is placed in a holder around the table. After each name is recited participants may, if they wish, share something that they feel made that sage special. This passing of the flame symbolizes the passing of the light of Torah and love of Zion throughout the generations. (Note that there are 39 candles in total.)].

GROUP

We invite the souls of the great scholars to our table:

PARTICIPANTS

We invite you:
Rabbi Akiva and Bruria
We invite you:
Rabbi Yochanan Ben Zakkai
We invite you:
Rabbi Yehuda HaNasi
We invite you:
Hillel and Shammai
We invite you:
Ravina
We invite you:
Ravashi
We invite you:
Rav Shrira Gaon
We invite you:
Rav Saadia Gaon
We invite you:
Rabbi Solomon Ben Issac, "Rashi"
We invite you:
Rav Jacob Meir, "Rabbeinu Tam"
We invite you:
Rav Solomon ben Aderet, "The Rashba"
We invite you:
Moses Ibn Ezra
We invite you:
Rabbi Moses ben Maimon, Maimonides or "The Rambam"
We invite you:
Judah HaLevi, "The Kuzari"
We invite you:
Moses Ben Nachman, "Nachmonides," or "The Ramban"
We invite you:
Moses De Leon
We invite you:
Solomon Alkabetz

We invite you:
Rav Jacob ben Moses Levi Loelin, or "The Maharal"
We invite you:
Rav Simon ben Tzemach Duran, or "The Rashbatz"
We invite you:
Rav Solomon ben Jehiel Luria, or "The Maharshal"
We invite you:
Rav Moses ben Joseph di Trani, or "The Mabit"
We invite you:
Rav Eliyahu ben Moses di Vidas, or "The Reishis Chochma"
We invite you:
Rav Joseph Caro
We invite you:
Issac Ben Solomon Luria, or the Ari,
We invite you:
The Baal Shem Tov
We invite you:
Rav Eliyahu ben Solomon Zalman, "The Vilna Gaon"
We invite you:
Rav Moses Sofer, the Chatam Sofer
We invite you:
Rav Solomon Ben Judah, the Maharshak
We invite you:
Rabbi Zecharya Frankel
(Founder of Conservative Movement)
Israel Jacobson
(Founder of Reform Movement)
We invite you:
Issac Weiss
(Founder of Hebrew Union College)
We invite you:
Gustav and Richard Gottheil,
We invite you:
Sabato Morais
(Founder of Jewish Theological Seminary)
We invite you:
Stephen Wise
We invite you:
Solomon Schecter

We invite you:
Martin Buber
We invite you:
Mordechai Kaplan
(Founder of Reconstructionist Judaism)
We invite you:
Judah Magnes[64]

GROUP

As we remember you, we are surrounded by many lights. The love you have shown in your life for our people, our Torah, and the land of Israel are the lights that surround us. This love kindles the flame of Zion that burned in our hearts for nearly 2,000 years as we awaited our return to the land.

PARTICIPANT

(Take Turns Reading)

It is your light, your spark that kindles the light of our soul. And it is your spark that inspires us and guides our path.

PARTICIPANT

Your thoughts and ideas have inspired our prayers, our liturgy, and the way we pray and observe Mitzvot even to this day.

PARTICIPANT

We look to you and seek your wisdom in our time of need. Your lives and your ideas help us find a way to bring peace to the blessed land of Israel and to our people. We know that your spark flickers when the flowers of the land begin to blossom.

PARTICIPANT

We invite you to join us and celebrate all of Israel's accomplishments. We invite you to celebrate the fulfillment of the dream, a 2,000-year-old dream to live in the land of our ancestors.

APPENDIX D

SPILLING WINE IN MEMORY OF THOSE WHO WERE KILLED IN SELF-DEFENSE

We thank G-d for enabling us to protect ourselves. We thank G-d that we have been victorious in fighting the wars waged against us, even though we are saddened that we have had to kill to protect ourselves. We are saddened that our enemy's lives have been ended as a result of defending ourselves from their attacks. For each war we have fought and for the ongoing war that the Palestinian leadership continues to wage against us, we spill a drop of wine to remember and to express our compassion for those we have killed in self-defense.

After reciting the name of each war, we spill a drop of wine on our plate or on our napkin to symbolically remove a drop of our happiness as we remember the lives that were ended.

War of Independence, 1948
Suez Campaign, 1956
Six-Day War, 1967
War of Attrition, 1969–1970
Yom Kippur War, 1973
Lebanon War, 1982
Intifada I, 1987
Intifada II, 2000—present day

APPENDIX E

PRAYER FOR ISRAELI SOLDIERS MISSING IN ACTION

May G-d who blessed our forefathers and foremothers—Abraham, Isaac, and Jacob, Sara, Rebecca, Rachel, and Leah—bless, preserve, and protect the captive and missing soldiers of the Israel Defense Forces.

May G-d rescue them from captivity and speedily restore them to peace and safety in the merit of our prayers of this holy assemblage of those who pray for them.

May G-d show them mercy, increase their strength, remove their pain, and grant them restoration of mind, body and spirit. May G-d return them to the bosom of their families swiftly and soon. [65]

APPENDIX F

I HOLD THE SEEDS OF ISRAEL'S FUTURE IN MY HANDS

Responsive Reading

LEADER

On May 15, 1948, the day Israel proclaimed its independence, the Secretary General of the Arab League, Azzam Pasha, proclaimed, "This will be a war of extermination and a momentous massacre which will be spoken of like the Mongolian Massacres and the Crusades." [66]

GROUP

But I hold the seeds to Israel's future in my hands.

LEADER

The Palestinian Leadership offered reconciliation with Israel and signed treaties written in English regarding shared use of land and promises to stop terrorism. To the International Community they used words of peace, while to their own people they proclaimed the following: "This is our Palestine from Metula (Israel's northern most border) to Rafiah (southern border) and to Aquaba (Israel's southern most point) from the (Jordan) River to the Mediterranean Sea; whether they want it or not." [67]

GROUP

But I hold the seeds to Israel's future in my hands.

LEADER

To the International Community, the Palestinian Leadership has publicly stated the quest for mutual respect and the hope of one day achieving a solution whereby two states—Israel and Palestine—can live peacefully as neighbors. In Arabic they have declared: "Allah willing, this unjust state,

Israel, will be erased; this unjust state, the United States, will be erased; this unjust state, Britain, will be erased...Blessing for whoever waged a Jihad for the sake of Allah. Blessings to whoever put a belt of explosives on his body or his son's and plunged into the midst of Jews." [68]

GROUP

But I hold the seeds to Israel's future in my hands.

We have encountered media and international policies biased against Israel. We have heard Palestinian leaders speaking words of peace in English while simultaneously calling for war and violence in Arabic. We know that international journalists slant their reports against Israel just so they can have the opportunity to interview Palestinian terrorists. We have watched how attacks against the United States are called acts of terrorism, while terrorists who commit the same acts against Jews living in Israel are referred to as "militants." We have seen the world accept and forgive the violence and murder committed daily against Jews while they condemn Israel for defending itself and attempting to uproot terrorist networks.[69]

GROUP

But I hold the seeds to Israel's future in my hands.

APPENDIX G

WINE PRODUCING REGIONS OF ISRAEL

Galilee/Golan

Including:
Lower Galilee
Upper Galilee
Tabor

Wines Grown in this Region
Chateau Golan
Galil Mountain
Galilee Mountain
Golan Heights Winery
Carmel Winery
Segal/Barkan Winery
Dalton Winery
Tabor
Recanati Winery
Yarden

Samaria
Mount Carmel
Sharon

Wines From This Region:
Carmel Winery at Zichron Yaakov
Margalit
Tishbi Winery
Saslove
Binyamina Winery

Shimshon –Samson

Wines From This Region
Barkan
Carmel Winery at Rishon LeZion
Segal Winery in Ramle
Karmei Yosef
Flam
Soreq

Judean Hills –Ha Rei Yehuda
Including the following towns:
Beth El
Jerusalem
Bethlehem
Hebron

Wines from this region
Castle at Ramat Raziel
Efrat at Motza
Clos De Gat
Sea Horse
Tzora
Efrat

The Negev
Ramat Arad–Upper Negev
Mitzpe Ramon–Central Negev

Wineries in this Region
Carmel at Ramat Arad
Barkan at Mitzpe Ramon[70]

APPENDIX H

EXPERIENTIAL USHPIZIN
(FOR CHILDREN AGES 3-12)

In this children's Ushpizin service, the children actually play the role of each holy guest.

Prior to the Seder, parents should read the letter on the following page to their children and prepare them for the Seder by reading and/or telling them about the major figures in Jewish History listed on the pages to follow. It will be important for children to understand who the figures are and why they were important to the Jewish people, the Jewish religion, and, most of all, to the modern State of Israel. The children will then be asked to pick one figure listed in the first Ushpizin and one listed in the second Ushpizin. The children are then encouraged to dress up in a costume that resembles one of the figures they chose and then role-play that figure at the Ushpizin.

Before starting the Ushpizin service, the children wait outside of the dining room. When the service starts and the exalted guests are called to the table, the children are invited into the dining room and are asked to tell the group who they are and why they are an important part of Jewish History.

The children are then asked to greet each person sitting at the table as that major figure in Jewish History. Participants sitting at the table are encouraged to give each child a small gift, such as a sweet candy, or a small toy. When the children have finished explaining who are they are, the rest of the Ushpizin is recited.

LETTER TO THE CHILDREN PARTICIPATING IN THE EXPERIENTIAL USHPIZIN

Dear Children,

Soon your family will be holding a special Seder with a dinner to celebrate Israel's birthday. While most birthdays are celebrated with close friends and a big birthday cake, this birthday is a little different because it celebrates a time when Jewish people were able to finally return to the land of Israel.

Have you ever gone away with your family on vacation for a week or a few days and thought about how much you missed being home? Can you imagine how much you would miss your home if you went away for two thousand years? Well, the Jewish people were away from their home for almost that much time.

If you were holding a birthday party for yourself, you would probably want all the people you love and care about to be there. Your friends and your family would be at the top of your list. Now that the country of Israel is having a birthday party we have to invite all of the people that are part of its family. Who is Israel's family? Well, the Jewish people of course. From the time the first Jew, who was named Abraham, came to the land of Israel (back then it was called Canaan) up to the Jews today who live in Israel, we are all part of one big family. There were many important Jews who helped the Jewish people and the land of Israel, but because we don't have time to mention them all, we can only mention a few. Here is the part where we need your help.

You will have a very important part in celebrating Israel's birthday party. The person who is reading this page to you will also read you a list of famous Jewish people. He or she will ask you to pick two famous Jewish people and say why you are picking those people. When the dinner starts you will have the chance to dress up like one of the people you picked and act like that person. You can teach everyone at the table about the person you picked simply by acting like them. When the grownups start the dinner, they will invite you into the dining room. When you walk into the dining room, you will be asked to walk up to each person at the table and show them your costume. Then you will tell them who you are and why you, as that famous person, are an important part of Jewish history.

There may even be a surprise for you if you do a good job.

I wish you a good Seder and hope you have lots of fun at this service.

Ushpizin of the Patriarchs and Matriarchs: The First Cup

Abraham
Abraham was the first Jew. He left his home in Ur and came to the land of Israel (back then it was called Canaan) where G-d gave the land to him and all of his children and children's children and so on. Abraham loved to have company, and he welcomed everyone who passed by to spend time with him in his tent.

Sarah
Sarah was a very beautiful woman. She was Abraham's wife, and she also had the courage to leave her home in Ur and travel with Abraham to a new land. She was also known to be a prophetess, which means that G-d spoke to her. Sarah did not give birth until she was very old, but when she finally did have a baby, she loved her son Isaac very much.

Isaac
Isaac is special because he was the first Jew to live his entire life in the land of Israel. Isaac was also willing to give up his life for G-d.

Rebecca
Rebecca was Isaac's wife, and she was very important in Jewish history. She knew that her son Esau was a hunter and was not interested in G-dly things. She also knew that Jacob was very interested in learning Torah and in following G-d's ways. Rebecca made sure that Isaac would give a special blessing to Jacob and not to Esau, even though Esau was the older son.

Jacob
Jacob was special because he wrestled with an angel and won, and for that reason he was given a new name, "Israel." Jacob also had two wives and two maid servants. Jacob worked fourteen years for his uncle Laban before he was allowed to marry. Jacob's children made up the twelve tribes of Israel.

Rachel
Rachel was a beautiful woman who was loved very much by her husband Jacob. Rachel prayed to G-d for children and later gave birth to Joseph and Benjamin.

Leah
Leah was Jacob's first wife and the mother of Reuben, Shimon, Levi, Zevulun, Issachar, and Judah.

Moses
Moses was the master prophet who was able to talk with G-d. Moses led the Children of Israel out of Egypt to Mount Nebo, which is right outside the land of Israel. He looked out over the land of Israel and dreamed about all of the wonderful things that would happen once the Jewish people got there.

Miriam
Miriam was the sister of Moses. G-d spoke to Miriam and told her what would happen in the future. Miriam helped Moses lead the Jewish people out of Egypt and helped him keep up their spirits while they wandered and waited in the Sinai desert until they were ready to enter the land of Israel.

Joshua
Joshua was very special because he led the Jewish people into the land of Israel and helped them form a new country.

Ushpizin for the Kingdom of Israel: The Second Cup

Deborah
Deborah was a prophetess, which means that G-d spoke to her. She saved the cities of Israel by leading the armies in a fight against Israel's enemies.

Ruth
Ruth was a kind and loving woman who was devoted to her family. Even though Ruth wasn't born Jewish she became Jewish and was very committed to living a Jewish life. She was so kind and loving that G-d decided to make Ruth's great-grandchild, David, the King of Israel. King David was the second King of Israel.

Hannah
Hannah was a prophetess and a special and holy woman. She prayed to G-d in a very special way. She spoke quietly to G-d with her eyes closed. It is because of Hannah that many of our prayers today are said silently.

Samuel
Samuel was the son of Hannah and a prophet. He was famous because he was given the job of declaring both King Saul and later King David "the King of Israel."

King Saul
King Saul was the first King of Israel. He spent much of his time defending Israel from people who were attacking it.

King David
King David was one of the holiest men who ever lived. He was a man who had tremendous courage. He made Jerusalem the capital of Israel and built up the Kingdom of Israel.

Bat Sheva
Bat Sheva married King David and was the mother of King Solomon.

King Solomon
King Solomon built the first Temple in Jerusalem. During his reign Israel was the biggest it had ever been. King Solomon had many friends, many wives, and was very wealthy and wise.

King Josiah

King Josiah hated idolatry and was very upset that so many Jewish people were worshiping idols. He encouraged his people to stop praying to idols and to start praying to G-d.

Nehemiah

Nehemiah led a large number of Jews from Babylon back to the land of Israel after the Persian King Cyrus allowed them to return. Nehemiah helped Ezra rebuild the Temple.

Ezra

Ezra was a scholar, who also led a large number of Jews back to the land of Israel and helped rebuild the Temple.

Judah Maccabee

Judah Maccabee defended the Jewish people from the Syrian Greek Empire, which was trying to make them less Jewish and more Greek. He was famous because he inspired other Jews to defend themselves and be proud of being Jewish.

Shimon Bar Kochba

Shimon Bar Kochba led the last major Jewish army in a revolt against the Roman Empire. He tried to keep the land of Israel under Jewish rule. Under his command the Jewish armies were able to keep the Roman armies out of many of Israel's towns and cities.

APPENDIX I

TIMELESS ZIONIST CONGRESS
(FOR TEENAGERS AND ADULTS)

(The purpose of this activity is to help participants become better acquainted with some of the most influential Zionist thinkers of the nineteenth and twentieth centuries. Its goal is *not* to re-create any particular Zionist Congress, but rather to bring to light the ideas of various Zionist thinkers from different periods of time. Each of the Zionists discussed in this activity were influential in making Israel a reality. Participants will learn about how these thinkers' ideas differed from one another and how each thinker had an impact on the present ideals of the State of Israel.)

LEADER

Imagine for a moment what it was like to live as a Jew in Europe in the late nineteenth century. The world was rapidly becoming industrialized, and movements of nationalism, Socialism and Darwinism, as well as, theories of the unconscious were first being popularized. In Western Europe Jews were living outside the shtetls (small Jewish communities) and had begun to work in all different parts of the secular world. However, in Eastern Europe and Russia there were new outbreaks of pogroms that killed many Jews. Because these mass murders of Jews were similar to those that occurred during the Middle Ages, Jewish people began to think differently about their future as a people living in the Diaspora. However, Jews had many different opinions about how they ought to pursue their future. Growing numbers of Jewish leaders and thinkers began to question whether the Jewish people had a future in Europe at all.

The first Zionist Congress was held in 1897 in Basel Switzerland to discuss the possibility of a Jewish homeland. Succeeding Zionist Congresses accomplished many great deeds, the most notable being the establishment of the State of Israel. In doing so they also contributed to the advancement of Jewish thought and culture. The following activity brings together many of the ideas developed by famous Zionist thinkers.

INSTRUCTIONS

On the page to follow, there is a brief description of each major Zionist ideology and some of the famous Zionist thinkers who held those beliefs. Briefly review that page and choose an ideology that is of interest to you. Go to the section which lists thinkers who held the ideology you chose. Once in the section review the description of the Zionist Thinkers and choose one famous Zionist Thinker whose ideas intrigue you.

Select one person who will begin this activity by reading the paragraph below, which calls the Zionist Congress to order.

After the congress is called to order Participants will go around the table taking turns reciting the quote from the Famous Zionist of their choice. The quotes are then briefly discussed by answering the follow up questions listed on the last page of this exercise.

Timeless Zionist Congress
A Guide to Famous Zionist Beliefs

To help you quickly select a quote of interest, please read the brief descriptions below of famous Zionist ideologies and choose one ideology you like. Then take a moment to review a few brief descriptions of famous Zionists who held those beliefs. Select one famous Zionist from that list. After the Zionist Congress has been called to order, the group will take turns reading the quotes they chose, and will discuss those quotes after they have finished.

Religious Zionism

The belief that a Jewish country must adhere to Jewish law and that the return of Jews from around the world to the land of Israel is the fulfillment of the process of redemption and the coming of the Messiah. The process of settling the land is seen as a fusion of "Torah V' Avodah" in other words fusing the commandments of the Torah with physical labor of the land. Proponents of this approach were: *Rabbi Avraham Kook, Rabbi Meir Bar-Ilan, Rabbi Samuel Mohilever, Rabbi Yehuda Alkalai, The Vilna Gaon, Yehiel Michael Pines and Solomon Schecter.*

Secular Zionism

Secular Zionism sees the need for a Jewish State coming not from the religious desire to bring the Messiah, but rather from the idea that the Jewish people need to be connected to and part of a growing Jewish culture where Jewish customs and principles are the norm. This culture cannot exist outside of a Jewish country. Also, Secular Zionists believe that a Jewish state is needed so that it can be a safe haven for Jews around the world who are subjected to Anti-Semitism. Secular Zionists were indifferent to where the Jewish State would be located. Argentina, Uganda, and Palestine were the areas in the world considered. Secular Zionist beliefs were held by many different famous Zionists in many different ways. Cultural Zionsim and Political Zionism were two forms of Secular Zionism which had a significant impact on the future of the State of Israel.

Cultural Zionism

Cultural Zionism is the belief that the Jewish people must modernize the Jewish culture and re-popularize the Hebrew language in order to make themselves ready for statehood. This process of cultural revival must be done through the work of a small selected group of people. Proponents of all or part of this belief were *Ahad Ha am (Asher Ginsberg), Chaim Nachman Bialik, Chaim Weitzmann, Martin Buber, Judah Leon Magnes, David Ben Gurion, Golda Meir, Aaron David Gordon.*

Political Zionism

Political Zionists believed that after so many centuries in exile, the Jewish people were still not considered equal citizens of any country where they lived. Political Zionists see Anti-Semitism as a historical reality and believed that if Jews remained without their own homeland they would forever be subjected to persecution and be lacking in power to stop it. Proponents of all or parts of this theory were: *Theodor Herzl, Louis Dembitz Brandeis, David Ben Gurion, Golda Meir, Max Nordau, Vladimir Jabotinsky, and Leon Pinsker.*[71]

Other Topics by Famous Zionists featured in the Quotes:

Dealing with the Local Arab population
Judah Leon Magnes
Vladimir Jabotinsky

Addressing the Social Problems in Palestine Pre-Statehood
Henrietta Szold

Love of the Land
Hannah Senesh

Calling the Zionist Congress to Order

PARTICIPANT

"Fellow Delegates: As one of those who called this Congress into being, I have been granted the privilege of welcoming you. We want to lay the cornerstone of the edifice that is one day to house the Jewish nation. The task is so great that we may treat it in none but the simplest terms. So far as we can now foresee, a summary of the present status of the Jewish question will be submitted within the coming three days." [72]

FAMOUS ZIONIST THINKERS ON THE FORMATION OF A JEWISH STATE

Religious Zionist Ideology

Jewish Mystical Approach to the Land of Israel
Avraham Kook (1864–1935)

Born in Latvia in 1864, Abraham Isaac Kook was well known to have deep insight and an unusually enlightened mind. Upon attending rabbinical seminary, Kook stood out from his classmates in his love of speaking Hebrew. After he served as a Rabbi in two different pulpits in Europe, his love of Zion drew him to the land of Israel. His approach to Zionism was based on Jewish mysticism, and his entire career was guided by these beliefs. He supported Religious Zionism over secular Zionism and saw Zionism as a way to bring about the Messianic era.

"Deep in the heart of every Jew in its purest and holiest recesses, there blazes the fire of Israel. There can be no mistaking its demands for an organic and indivisible bond between life and all of G-d's commandments: for the pouring of the spirit of the L-rd, the spirit of Israel which completely permeates the soul of the Jew into all the vessels which were created for this particular purpose, and for expressing the word Israel fully and precisely in the realms of action and idea.

In the hearts of our saints this fire is constantly blazing up with tongues of holy flame. Like the fire on the altar of the temple it is burning unceasingly with a steady flame in the collective heart of our people. Hidden away in the deepest recesses of their souls, it exists even among the backsliders and sinners of Israel. Within the Jewish people as a whole this is the living source of its desire for freedom, of its longing for a life worthy of the name for man and community, of its hope for redemption, of the striving toward a full, uncontradictory, and unbounded Jewish life...."This is the meaning of the Jew's undying love for Eretz Israel— the land of holiness, the land of G-d in which all of the Divine commandments are realized in their perfect form."[73]

Religious Zionism
Rabbi Meir Bar-Ilan (1880–1949)

Born in Lithuania, Rabbi Bar-Ilan became a devoted religious Zionist by the age of 22. He was deeply committed to building Jewish settlements in the Holy Land and believed that a future Jewish State should be both modern and committed to observance of Jewish law. Rabbi Bar Ilan moved to Israel in 1926 and became the International Head of the Mizrachi movement. He devoted his life to Religious Zionism and to resolving the cultural differences between secular and observant Jews, but ultimately he hoped to transition the society towards one being governed by Jewish Law.

"A 'new' problem is now arising among us, the question of Church and State....Church and State are kept separate and treated as separate provinces. Clergymen and civil judges have separate duties covering different spheres, and one does not encroach upon the domain of the other.

Our case is different. Our Torah and traditions are not a man-made constitution but G-d's own law. If we say, 'this law is good, this one is not,' we negate everything...There is a general principle as to how society developed....First, people migrated to a country individually and in groups. Then, they organized for various activities, and out of their private and social lives they evolved customs and mores... If this process was obtained today as well, our return to our homeland would be very difficult... How shall we integrate the laws of our ancestral heritage with the customs and outlooks to which we have become accustomed in the various lands of our dispersion?...There will be many coming to Eretz Israel, especially from Europe and America who, though in general sympathy with Judaism, are not at all familiar with the Torah. These will say, 'What are the laws of the Jewish tradition to us? Let each man and every group live by its own customs and traditions. Later when things are stabilized, the situation will be ready for the work of the lawmakers. They will choose the best and worthiest practices from among all those that will exist and formulate them as laws'.... In opposition to this opinion another kind of extremist may maintain that modern customs and conditions are to be ignored entirely. 'We must live only according to the laws of our Torah, and it is irrelevant to us that many people do not understand its laws or know their meaning. We recommend our way, the third approach, as the solution to this conflict. It is our conviction that there can be no substitute for the Torah. This does not mean that we should scoff at or ignore the customs of this generation. Even if these values and customs are in contradiction to the laws of the Torah, we must modify them gradually. We have to begin our task not with passing laws but by educating the young and by influencing their elders." [74]

Religious Zionism
Rabbi Samuel Mohilever (1824–98)

Rabbi Samuel Mohilever was born in the early part of the nineteenth century in a village near Vilna, the Jewish intellectual capital of Lithuania. He was ordained at the age of 18 because of his wisdom in the Torah. Rabbi Mohilever played a fundamental role in the development of Religious Zionism in Russia and in unifying Orthodox and Secular Zionists toward the goal of creating a Jewish State in Palestine. He also persuaded Baron Edmond De Rothschild to support the settlement of Jews in the Holy Land, settlements which Rothschild continued to support until his death in 1934.

"It is essential that the Congress unite all 'Sons of Zion' who are true to our cause to work in complete harmony and fraternity, even if there be among them differences of opinion regarding religion.

All Sons of Zion must be completely convinced and must believe with a perfect faith that the resettlement of our country, i.e.; the purchase of land and the building of houses, the planting of orchards, and the cultivation of the soil, is one of the fundamental commandments of our Torah.

The basis of Hibbat Zion is the Torah, as it has been handed down to us from generation to generation with neither supplement nor subtraction.

Our task is to build and to plant and not tear down and destroy....We must dispatch compelling speakers to all the lands of the Diaspora to spread our cause among our people and gain their support.

As for the national Trust, we must make every effort to persuade the directors of the Jewish Colonization Association to set aside a great portion of the monies under their control for the resettlement of the Holy Land.

In conclusion, I lift my voice to my brethren: Behold it is now 2,000 years that we await our Messiah, to redeem us from our bitter exile and to gather our scattered brethren from all corners of the earth to our own land where each shall dwell in security, under his vine and under his fig tree."[75]

Religious Zionism
Rabbi Yehuda Alkalai (1798–1878)
Born in Sarajevo at the end of the eighteenth century, Rabbi Yehuda Alkalai never lived to see the first Zionist Congress, but his ideas laid the foundation for the Zionists of the latter nineteenth century. Rabbi Alkalai lived in Jerusalem where he was influenced by the Kabbalists of the time. He believed that the Jewish people could begin the process of bringing Moshiach (the Messiah) by taking the land of Israel in a military battle. He was also the first to propose the idea that there needs to be a 'great assembly' of Jews to form an organization that could purchase the land of Israel, an idea later adopted by Theodor Herzl that led to the establishment of the Jewish National Fund.

"It is written in the Bible: 'Return O L-rd unto the tens and thousands of families of Israel.' On this verse the Rabbis commented in the Talmud as follows: it proves that the Divine Presence can be felt only if there are at least two thousand and two tens of thousands of Israelites together. Yet we pray every day: 'Let our eyes behold thy return in mercy unto Zion.' Upon whom should the Divine Presence rest? On sticks and stones? Therefore, as the first step in the redemption of our souls we must cause at least 22,000 to return to the Holy Land. This is the necessary preparation for a descent of the Divine Presence among us: afterward, He will grant us and all Israel further signs of his favor...

Undoubtedly our greatest wish is to gather our exiles from the four corners of the earth to become one bond. We are, alas, so scattered and divided today because each Jewish community speaks a different language and has different customs. These divisions are an obstacle to the redemption....The redemption will begin with efforts by the Jews themselves; they must organize and unite, choose leaders, and leave the lands of exile....Once the name of Israel is again applied to our land, all Jews will be inspired to help this company with all the means at their disposal. Though this venture will begin modestly, its future will be great."[76]

Religious Zionism
Solomon Schecter (1847–1915)

Solomon Schecter was born in Romania, and while he never took an active role in the Zionist movement, he had a great impact on American Zionism. During his 14-year position as Chancellor of the Jewish Theological Seminary in New York he was mainly responsible for inspiring the American Conservative movement to be the most overwhelmingly supportive of Zionism of the three major Jewish religious branches in the United States.

"I belong to the class of Zionists that lays more stress on the religious-national aspects of Zionism than on any other feature peculiar to it. The rebirth of Israel's national consciousness and the revival of Israel's religion, or, to use a shorter term, the revival of Judaism, are inseparable. When Israel found itself, it found its G-d. When Israel lost itself, or began to work at its self–effacement, it was sure to deny its G-d. The selection of Israel, the indestructibility of G-d's covenant with Israel, the immortality of Israel as a nation, and the final restoration of Israel to Palestine, where the nation will live a holy life on holy ground...all these are common ideals."[77]

Religious Zionism
The Vilna Gaon (1720–97)

Rabbi Elijah, the Vilna Gaon ("the Genius from Vilna"), was born almost 180 years before the first Zionist Congress. However, his influence on modern Zionism was great since he was responsible for increasing support for Jewish settlements in the land of Israel as a way to bring forth the Messianic Era. In his quotation that follows he states that in order to begin the Messianic Era there needs to be at least 600,000 Jews living in the Holy Land, which was exactly the number of Jews living in Israel on the day the state declared its independence.

"We must bring 600,000 Jews to the Land of Israel. That number will be decisive. Indeed, at the time of the Exodus from Egypt 600,000 left that place. There is also a special blessing in the prayer book to be recited when one sees 600,000 Jews assembled in the same place....Then our God, who promised the Land of Israel to our ancestors and who promised that their descendants would live there in security, will bring more and more Jews there." [78]

Secular Zionism vs. Religious Zionism
Yehiel Michael Pines (1842–1912)

Yehiel Michael Pines, who was born in Grodno in 1842, was known as an Orthodox Jew who was in touch with the secular world. He held that Jewish national identity was unique because it was based in religion. To Pines, the notion of a Jewish nation that was not Jewish in its observance of religion was an impossible idea.

"I have no sympathy with the currently fashionable movement to make the Jewish people a purely secular nationality in place of the combination of religion with nationality that has enabled us to survive to this day.

Whatever merit there may be to this theory, it is to be found only in its possible value as applied to the assimilated Jews, that is to those de-Judaized individuals who have remained members of the Jewish faith in name only and are ready to drop out of the Jewish community. Such Jews may find in the idea of secular Jewish nationality a new bond to reinforce their attachment to their people. But I see a strong tendency these days, one fostered by a well-known school of thought, to impose the idea of secular nationalism on the whole Jewish people, including pious Jews, to try to separate religion from nationality, and to make the latter a self-sufficient entity upon which Jewish survival is to depend. It is against this that I rise in vigorous opposition, for in the consequences of this doctrine I can see nothing but incalculable harm. It is as if one were to try to deprive a living body of its soul in order to revive it by an electric shock, which may have value in resuscitation, but there is no substitute for real vitality."[79]

Secular Zionist Thinkers

Secular Zionism through the Growth of Jewish Culture
Ahad Ha'Am (1856–1927)

Asher Ginzberg was born in Russia where he was a scholar of both Talmud and Chassidic literature. He slowly became influenced by the literary works of the Haskala (the Jewish Enlightenment) and became enthralled with the ideas of Maimonides. He was later influenced by Russian Positivism and ceased his religious observance. Ginsberg became the editor for a Hebrew monthly called Ha Shiloah and later left the paper and moved, first to London, then to Palestine. He became involved in the Hibbat Zion movement and began writing again under the Hebrew name of Ahad Ha'Am. Ginzberg stressed the importance of creating a cultural revival and modernization of the Jewish people through the work of a carefully selected small group of people. The new Jewish spiritual culture he proposed was agnostic (uncertain about G-d's existence). His work inspired the organization of the Bnei-Moshe movement, which sought to raise the moral and cultural component of the work involved in reviving the Jewish nation. Although Ahad Ha'Am attended only the first Zionist Congress and never accepted a leadership position, his work inspired many great Israeli leaders and thinkers.

"True Hibbat Zion is not merely a part of Judaism, nor is it something added onto Judaism; it is the whole of Judaism, but with a different focal point. Hibbat Zion neither excludes the written word nor seeks to modify it artificially by addition or subtraction. It stands for a Judaism which shall have as its focal point the ideal of our nation's unity, its renascence, and its free development through expression of universal human values in the terms of its own distinct spirit.

This is the conception of Judaism on which our education and our literature must be based. We must revitalize the idea of our national renascence and use every possible means to strengthen its hold and deepen its roots, until it becomes an organic element in the Jewish consciousness and an independent dynamic force. Only in that way, it seems to me, can the Jewish soul be freed from its shackles and regain contact with the broad stream of human life without having to pay for its freedom by the sacrifice of its individuality."[80]

Secular Zionism through the Growth of Jewish Culture
Chaim Nachman Bialik (1873–1934)

Chaim Nachman Bialik, who was born in Volhynia, was influenced by the turmoil of Russian Jewish life in the late nineteenth century. He was inspired by the works of other contemporary Zionist thinkers and became well known as a master of a new form of Hebrew poetry, inspired by the ideology and influenced by Ahad Ha'Am, but he was more spiritually connected to the Jewish past. He also stressed the need to preserve classical Hebrew as a "usable past."

"We have come to the conclusion that a people that aspires to a dignified existence must create a culture; it is not enough merely to make use of a culture. A people must create its own, with its own hands and its own implements and materials and impress it with its own seal. Of course, our people in its Diasporas are creating culture; I doubt whether any place in the world where culture is being produced is entirely devoid of Jews. But as whatever the Jew creates in the Diaspora is always absorbed in the culture of others, it loses its identity and is never accounted to the credit of a Jew. Our cultural account in the Diaspora is consequently all debit and no credit. The Jewish people is therefore in a painfully false position: Whereas its true function culturally is that of a proletariat (i.e.; it produces with the materials and implements of others for others), it is regarded by others and at times even by itself as a cultural parasite, possessing nothing of its own. A self- respecting people will never become reconciled to such a lot; it is bound to arise one day and resolve: No more. Better a little that is undisputedly my own than much that is not definitely either mine or someone else's. Better a dry crust in my own home and on my own table than a stalled-fed ox in the home of others and on the table of others." [81]

Secular Zionism Built through Diplomacy
Chaim Weizmann (1874–1952)

Chaim Weizmann, who was born in Russia but later moved to England and became a British citizen, was one of the most influential Jewish leaders of the twentieth century, as well as a leading scientist of his day. Although he was an ardent supporter of Herzl, he opposed his concept of political Zionism and supported Jewish cultural colonization of Palestine. Weitzman advised the British on the Jewish national interests in the land of Palestine and also became the first president of the World Zionist Organization. He met with people in the highest political circles, using diplomacy as a way to gain a state. However, his gradualist approach to the establishment of the State of Israel was later rejected by Ben-Gurion.

"Now we have an address, a name, and above all, great moral credit. Now we can build and now we can demand, now is the time. The time is approaching for greater activity on the part of the British government, because it has been convinced that we mean business. Although many Jewish notables are not with us, the British government knows that we have the necessary strength for the work of reconstruction. A great deal of educational work was necessary for that. If you say there are Arabs but we must get rid of them, there is Britain, but we must force it, then you may be playing the part of the contrabass in an orchestra, but it will never make a song. Of this I am firmly convinced."[82]

Zionism through the Growth and Development of a Jewish Culture
Martin Buber (1878–1965)

Martin Buber was born in Vienna and educated at German universities. Although he taught philosophy and religion at the University of Frankfurt, he was influenced mostly by Chasidic Jewish thought and became an active Zionist. He worked under Theodor Herzl as editor of Die Welt, the official Zionist publication of the time, but he left because of political differences since he believed more in cultural Zionism than in political Zionism. Buber moved to Palestine in 1938 and was the chair of the Social Philosophy Department at Hebrew University in Jerusalem. He also joined Judah Magnes in advocating for a bi-national state. His ideology was based on Hegel, Berdichevski (another famous Zionist thinker), and Nietzsche's vision of a new society. He believed that the Jews' capacity for morality and for answering the demands of G-d through Zionism was the source of their greatness as a people. He believed that the land of Israel held a unique opportunity for achieving greatness.

"I am setting up Hebrew Humanism in opposition to that Jewish nationalism which regards Israel as a nation like unto other nations and recognizes no task for Israel save that of preserving and asserting itself. But no nation in the world has this as its only task, for just as an individual who wishes merely to preserve and assert himself leads an unjustified and meaningless existence, so a nation with no other aim deserves to pass away....

Israel is not a nation like other nations, no matter how much its representatives have wished it during certain eras. Israel is a people like no other, for it is the only people in the world which from its earliest beginnings has been both a nation and a religious community.... Thanks to the unparalleled work in Palestine, the nation is on the rise. The religion, however, is on a steep downward fall, for it is no longer a power which determines all of life; it has been confined to the special sphere of ritual and sermons. But a Jewish nation cannot exist without religion any more than a Jewish religious community without nationality. Our only salvation is to become Israel again, to become a whole, the unique whole of a people and a religious community; a renewed people, a renewed religion, and the renewed unity of both."[83]

Secular Zionism and Jewish Nationalism
Leo Pinsker (1821–91)

Leo Pinsker was the most assimilated of the Russian Jewish Zionists. He received a secular education, attended medical school in Moscow, and later practiced medicine in Odessa. In reaction to the pogroms, he adopted a more Zionist belief. He wrote the book, "Auto Emancipation," in which he advocated that Jewish nationalism was the antidote to anti-Semitism.

"If we would have a secure home, so that we may give up our endless life of wandering and rehabilitate our nation in our own eyes and in the eyes of the world, we must above all not dream of restoring ancient Judea. We must not attach ourselves to the place where our political life was once violently interrupted and destroyed. The goal of our present endeavors must not be the "holy land," but a land of our own. We need nothing but a large piece of land for our poor brothers, a piece of land which shall remain our property from which no foreign master can expel us. Thither we shall take with us the most sacred possessions which we have saved from the shipwreck of our former fatherland, the G-d idea and the Bible. It is only these which have made our old fatherland the Holy Land.... Perhaps the Holy Land will again become ours. If so, all the better, but first of all we must determine—and this is the crucial point—what country is accessible to us, and at the same time adapted to offer Jews of all lands who must leave their homes a secure and unquestioned refuge which is capable of being made productive."[84]

Secular Zionism: The Formation of a Country
Judah Leon Magnes (1877–1948)

Born in San Francisco in 1877 and a graduate of the Reform Rabbinical Seminary at Hebrew Union College in Cincinnati, Magnes became the associate Rabbi of the Reform Congregation Temple Emanuel in New York City and Rabbi of the Conservative Congregation B'nai Jeshurun, also in New York City. However, he left both congregations due to their religious liberalism and started The Society for the Advancement of Judaism in 1920. He was a fervent believer in the ideas of Ahad Ha'Am, but he saw them in a religious context. He believed in the spiritual rebirth of Israel as the true meaning of Zionism. He was best known for being the first Chancellor of Hebrew University in Jerusalem. Politically, he doubted that a Jewish State could be established in Palestine and believed that a bi-national state would be more viable.

Ideology

"What is our Zionism? What does Palestine mean for us? As to what we should want here, I can answer for myself in almost the same terms that I have been in the habit of using many years: Immigration. Settlement of the land. Hebrew life and Culture.

If you guarantee these for me, I should be willing to yield the Jewish State, and the Jewish majority; and on the other hand I would agree to a legislative assembly together with a democratic political regime so carefully planned and worked out that the above three fundamentals could not be infringed. Indeed, I should be willing to pay almost any price for these three, especially since this price would in my opinion also secure tranquility and mutual understanding."[85]

On Dealing with Local Arab Populations

"What I am driving at is to distinguish between two policies. The one maintains that we can establish a Jewish Home here through the suppression of the political aspirations of the Arabs, and therefore a Home necessarily established on bayonets over a long period—a policy which I think bound to fail because of the violence against us it would occasion and because good opinion in Britain and the conscience of the Jewish people itself would revolt against it. The other policy holds that we can establish a Home here only if we are true to ourselves as democrats and internationalists, thus being just and helpful to others, and that we ask for the protection of life and property while we are eagerly and intelligently and sincerely at work to find *modus vivendi et operandi* with our neighbors."[86]

Political Zionism
Louis Dembitz Brandeis (1856–941)
Louis Brandeis was born in Louisville, Kentucky and served 22 years on the U.S. Supreme Court. He had no religious connection to Judaism until the age of 54 when he was called to New York to help settle a strike in the mostly Jewish garment workers industry. While there, Brandeis met Jacob Haas, who had been originally part of Theodor Herzl's core leadership. Brandeis became an active member in the Federation of American Zionists. He supported the building of Palestine on a national basis and not a cultural one.

"Let us bear in mind what Zionism is…It is essentially a movement to give the Jew more, not less freedom; it aims to enable the Jews to exercise the same right now exercised by practically every other people in the world; to live at their option either in the land of their fathers or in some other country…Let no American imagine that Zionism is inconsistent with Patriotism. Multiple loyalties are objectionable only if they are inconsistent. A man is a better citizen of the United States for being also a loyal citizen of his state, and of his city; for being loyal to his family, and to his profession or trade; for being loyal to his college or his lodge... Every American Jew who aids in advancing the Jewish settlement in Palestine, though he feels that neither he nor his descendants will ever live there, will likewise be a better man and a better American for doing so.... There is no inconsistency between loyalty to America and loyalty to Jewry. The Jewish spirit, the product of our religion and experiences is essentially modern and essentially American."[87]

Political/ Secular Zionism:
The Importance of Unity in Building a Jewish Nation
David Ben-Gurion (1886–1973)

David Ben-Gurion was born in Poland where his family was devoted to the Zionist movement. He immigrated to Palestine in 1903 and quickly rose to the leadership of the labor unions and then the overall Zionist movement. Ben Gurion later became Israel's first Prime Minister. He stressed the importance of Jewish unity and saw the Jewish labor union workers as the ideal building blocks of the Jewish State. While he was strongly opposed to many of the ideas expressed by Vladimir Jabotinsky (to be discussed later), he adopted some of them, particularly those relating to the establishment of Jewish defense.

"Unity is the imperative of our mission and our destiny. Nonetheless, of all the values of our movement it is the one that is perhaps most honored in theory and least respected in practice. We may now be attempting to become rooted in the homeland and laboring to create an independent life, but the habits of disunity and anarchy which grew wild among us in the course of hundreds of years of exile and subservience cannot easily be corrected....The Jewish Revolution requires not only an undivided and organic partnership of all the workers in Israel but also the mutual co-operation of the labor and the nation...The absorption of immigrants will be a more difficult task than ever before and will require of us new and unprecedented efforts. The new immigrants will be coming to us from misery and poverty and will need prolonged care and intensive help from the pioneer vanguard."[88]

Political Secular Zionism
Golda Meir (1898–1978)

Golda Meir was the fourth Prime Minister of Israel (and the first female leader of the State of Israel) and was very influential in its establishment. She was born in Kiev, Russia in 1898 and emigrated with her family to the United States when she was eight years old. They settled in Milwaukee, Wisconsin, where Golda became a school-teacher and involved herself in the Zionist labor movement. In 1921 she moved to Palestine with her husband and sister. Golda immediately became influential in labor union disputes, and her success resulted in her ascent to higher and higher levels of appointed and elected positions. During her tenure as Prime Minister, Golda strengthened US support for Israel, encouraged the immigration of thousands of Jews from Russia to Israel, and supported Israel's aid to a variety of African nations.

"To attain peace, I am ready to go at any hour to any place, to meet any authorized leader of any Arab State—to conduct negotiations with mutual respect, in parity and without pre-conditions, and with a clear recognition that the problems under controversy can be solved. For there is room to fulfill the national aspirations of all the Arab States and of Israel as well in the Middle East, and progress, development and cooperation can be hastened among all its nations, in place of barren bloodshed and war without end.

If peace does not yet reign, it is from no lack of willingness on our part: it is the inevitable outcome of the refusal of the Arab leadership to make peace with us. That refusal is still a projection of reluctance to be reconciled to the living presence of Israel within secure and recognized boundaries, still a product of the hope, which flickers on in their hearts, that they will accomplish its destruction. And this has been the state of things since 1948, long before the issue of the territories arose in the aftermath of the Six-Day War."[89]

Political Secular Zionism
Max Nordau (1849–1923)

Born in Hungary in 1849, Max Nordau was Theodor Herzl's friend and most important colleague. He was also a writer and was well known for being a social critic. Nordau was influenced by many of the late nineteenth century theories about mental health and used many of these theories in his writings.

"The Zionists know that they have undertaken a work of unparalleled difficulty. Never before has the effort been made to transplant several million people peacefully and in a short space of time from various countries; never has the attempt been made to transform millions of physically degenerate proletarians without trade or profession into farmers and herdsmen; to bring town-bred hucksters and tradesmen, clerks and men of sedentary occupation, into contact again with the plough and with mother earth. It will be necessary to get Jews of different origins to adjust to one another, to train them practically for national unity, and at the same time to overcome the superhuman obstacles of different language, cultural level, ways of thought, and varying prejudices of people who will come to Palestine from all countries of the world.

What gives Zionists the courage to begin this labor of Hercules is the conviction that they are performing a necessary and useful task, a work of love and civilization, a work of justice and wisdom. They wish to save eight to ten million of their kin from intolerable suffering...They wish to deprive anti-Semitism, which lowers the morals of the community everywhere and develops the very worst instincts of its victims...They wish to make Jews who are nowadays reproached for being parasites into an undeniably productive people. They desire to irrigate with their sweat and to till with their hands a country that is today desert until it again becomes the blooming garden it once was."[90]

Political Secular Zionism
Theodor Herzl (1860–1904)

Theodor Herzl was the father of modern Zionism. He was educated as a lawyer, but then he became a journalist, earning fame for his essays and plays. He was later hired by Neue Freie Presses; the most highly regarded Viennese newspaper, and sent to Paris as a correspondent. His interest in Zionism arose after he reported on the trial of Alfred

Dreyfus, a Jewish army captain with the French General staff who was accused of spying for Germany. Although the case against Dreyfus was unfounded, Dreyfus was stripped of his rank and faced mobs shouting anti-Semitic slurs. This experience transformed Herzl and made him committed to to the Zionist cause.

"Can we wait in pious resignation till the princes and peoples of the earth are more mercifully disposed toward us? I say that we cannot hope for the current to shift. And why not? Even if we were near to the hearts of princes as are their other subjects, they could not protect us. They would only incur popular hatred by showing us too much favor. And this "too much" implies less than is claimed as a right by any ordinary citizen or ethnic group....Let sovereignty be granted us over a portion of the globe adequate to meet our rightful national requirements; we will attend to the rest.

To create a state is neither ridiculous nor impossible...we must not visualize the exodus of the Jews as a sudden one. It will be gradual, proceeding over a period of decades. Is Palestine or Argentina preferable? The society will take whatever it is given and whatever the Jewish public opinion favors. The society will determine both these points...Let me repeat once more my opening words: The Jews who will it shall achieve their state. We shall live at last as free men on our own soil, and in our own homes peacefully die."[91]

Jewish Nation Building, Jewish Self Defense
Vladimir Jabotinsky (1880-1940)
Vladimir Jabotinsky was born in Odessa, Russia, and after graduating from high school became a writer for various newspapers. He became an active Zionist in 1903, when he assisted in organizing a Jewish defense corps to defend against a potential pogrom. He was a well-known orator and soon focused his talent on promoting the idea of Zionism. He believed that Zionism meant a bold political struggle for a state. He did not believe that the Turkish government or the Arabs who lived in Palestine at the time would adapt to the Zionists and their push for a government. Rather, Jewish political achievements and Jewish power were the only way to achieve statehood. Jabotinsky believed in the mass immigration of Jews to Palestine and in establishing Jewish police and military units to protect local Jewish populations

from harm. This belief differed from that of Chaim Weitzmann, who held that no action toward statehood should be taken without British consent. Jabotinsky's ideology laid the foundation for the Betar movement. In the quotation that follows he also comments on the issue of dealing with the local Arab population.

Ideology

"The duty and aim of Betar is very simple though difficult: to create that type of Jew which the nation needs in order to better and quicker build a Jewish state. In other words, to create a 'normal,' 'healthy' citizen for the Jewish nation. The greatest difficulty is encountered because as a nation the Jews today are neither 'normal' nor 'healthy' and life in Diaspora affects the intelligent upbringing of normal and healthy citizens.

During 2,000 years of exile the Jewish nation lost the habit of concentrating its will power on an all-important task, lost the habit of acting in unison as a people, lost the ability to defend itself; armed in case of emergency, instead, the Jews became accustomed to shouts rather than deeds, to disorder and disorganization, to negligence both in social and personal life. Every step of the Betar education signifies, therefore, a desire to reach the top and achieve this 'normalcy' even though it will take a long time for every Betari to grow up in the proper ways of life and behavior.

The basis of the Betarian viewpoint consists of one idea: the Jewish State. In this simple idea, however, lies a deep meaning indeed. What do the nations of the world symbolize? They symbolize that every nation must contribute its own share to the common culture of mankind, a share which is distinguished by its own specific spirit. This contribution should not and cannot consist merely of the ideas and good advice to other nations; it must serve as a living example of ideas and ideals, tangibly realized, expressed not only in books but in the collective life of the people as well. For this purpose every nation must possess its own 'laboratory,' a country wherein the nation alone is master and can freely suit the common life in accordance with its own conception of good and evil. A people's own state is such a laboratory."[92]

Dealing with the Local Arab Populations

"We maintain unanimously that the economic position of the Palestinian Arabs under the Jewish colonization and owing to the Jewish colonization has become the object of envy in all the surrounding Arab countries, so that the Arabs from those countries show a clear tendency to immigrate to Palestine.... The Arabs of Palestine will necessarily become a minority in the country of Palestine. What I do deny is that that is a hardship. It is not a hardship on any race, any nation, possessing so many national states now and so many more National States in the future. One fraction, one branch of that race, and not a big one, will have to live in someone else's state.... When the Arab claim is confronted with our Jewish demand to be saved, it is like the claims of appetite versus the claims of starvation."[93]

Development of the Land of Israel

The Purpose of Jewish Nationalism
Aaron David Gordon (1856–1922)

Aaron David Gordon was born in the province of Podolia, Russia to a well known family. He later became known as the Zionist movement's secular mystic. He first emigrated in 1904 at the age of 47 to Petach Tikva where he found day labor in a vineyard. Previously a white-collar worker, Gordon held the belief that redemption could come only through physical labor. His writing stressed the importance and sanctity of working the land of Israel. Much of his writing was influenced by the Kabbalists when he emphasized the mystical and metaphysical bonds between the Jew and the land of Israel.

"I think that everyone of us ought to retreat for a moment into his innermost self... and then ask himself with the utmost simplicity, seriousness and honesty: what essentially is the purpose of our national movement? What do we expect to find in Palestine that no other place can give us? Why should we segregate ourselves from the nations among whom we have lived our lives? In other words, why should we not completely assimilate ourselves among those nations? What stops us? It seems that every one of us can answer this question... That answer is that there is a primal force inside every one of us which is fighting for its own life, which seeks its own realization.

Jewish life in the Diaspora lacks this cosmic element of national identity; it is sustained by the historic element alone, which keeps us alive and will not let us die, but it cannot provide us with a full national life... In the countries of the Galut (Diaspora) we are compelled to lead an inanimate existence, lacking in national creativity (and from the point of view of genuine personality also lacking in individual creativity). There we are the dependents of others materially and perhaps even more spiritually.... It is life we want, no more and no less than that, our own life feeding our own vital sources, in the fields and under the skies of our homeland, a life based on our own physical and mental labors."[94]

Love of the Land of Israel

Hannah Senesh (1921–1943?)
Hannah Senesh, who was born in 1921 in Budapest, Hungary, demonstrated a remarkable literary talent at a young age. She came from an assimilated family, but due to the anti-Semitic sentiment in Europe at the time, she became involved in Zionist activism and left Hungary for the Holy Land at the age of 19. In 1943 Senesh joined the British Army and volunteered to be parachuted behind German lines to make contact with the Jewish partisans, who were resisting the Nazis. Caught by the Hungarian police, she was tortured for information and then executed. Her life and poetry became symbols of idealism and self-sacrifice.

"It is my second visit to Caesarea and I am even more impressed than the first time. When you are on the seashore, you recall the past, you think of the future. The horizon seems to open before you and you feel more determined than ever to accomplish something great and beautiful. For various reasons, the atmosphere in the kibbutz is now more intimate and more harmonious. In the morning, I roam through the ancient ruins; in the afternoon, I walk in the fields, or to be more precise, on the land designated to become our fields. When I see with what fury the foamy waves rush against the shore and how they become silent and peaceful upon crashing against the sand, I think that our enthusiasm and anger is not much different. As they roll, they are powerful and vigorous and when they touch the shore, they break, they calm down and they begin to play like small children on the golden sand."[95]

Addressing the Social Problems in the Formation of a Jewish Nation
Henrietta Szold (1860–1945)

The founder of Hadassah, Henrietta Szold, was an American educator, author, and social worker. In her home town of Baltimore, she became involved in the Americanization of Russian-Jewish immigrants, later opening a night school for them. In 1897 she joined the Zionist Association of Baltimore. In 1907 Henrietta was invited to join the Hadassah Study circle, which later became Hadassah—the Women's Zionist Organization America movement. Through her work she organized the American Zionist Medical Unit, which trained nurses, and became the honorary president of Hadassah and part of the executive branch of the World Zionist Organization. She also became the director of the Youth Aliyah Agency, which saved thousand of Jewish children from Nazi Germany and other European countries.

"The universal truism takes on vivid coloring in a country of immigration, and in an immigration country par excellence like Jewish Palestine-in-the-building, the welfare of the child must be regarded as a consuming, ever present task. Jewish Palestine is faced with the unique duty of effecting a double synthesis, the synthesis between the Jewish past and the Jewish present, and the synthesis among the fragments, the jetsam and flotsam, of World Jewry that make up "the gathering of the exiles." The Jewish groups which partly seep, partly are catapulted into Palestine from the Asiatic East must make the painful adjustment of static habits and the psychology of a past epoch to advanced modern standards coupled with a hectic progressiveness that brooks no delay. The process hews a wide cleft between parents left behind in the race and the children oblivious of the pangs of adjustment. They, the parents and their children, do not speak the same language; they have different behavior standards; they stand opposed to each other not only with the traditional antagonism of fathers and sons. There is the added virus injected by the total lack of comprehension on the side of the bewildered elders and lack of filial reverence on the side of the youngsters. Parental authority is lost in the shuffle, and long unutilized national talents among the Yemenites, the Persians, the Bukharians, among all the fragments coming together to form a reconstituted body, continue to lie dormant, unexploited."[96]

Timeless Zionist Congress
Follow-Up Questions to be Discussed
After the Delegates Have Spoken

After all participants have read their quotes, they answer and discuss the following questions:

1. Why did you choose that person?

2. Do you agree or disagree with that person's views? Why or why not?

3. Do you think that the person you chose would still hold the same belief if he or she were alive today?

4. What questions do you have for other participants about the quotes they chose to read?

APPENDIX J

PERSONAL Y'HI RATZON FOR THE STATE OF ISRAEL

For Children and Adults

This Year I Wish for Israel....

Each participant states aloud one wish that he or she has for Israel in the upcoming year. Each participant then writes that wish in the space below (if the participant is not able to write, then an adult can write the wish for that participant. Next to that wish, the person writes his or her name and the date. When this Seder is held again next year, the person holding this Haggadah will see the wish that was written in the previous year and who wrote it. With each year that passes Israel's growth will be documented in these Haggadot (Seder books) through the hopes of the Jewish people who celebrate Israel's independence by participating in this Seder.

"May it be the will of G-d in the upcoming year to:

_____

_____

_____

_____

_____

_____

_____

APPENDIX K

Arts and Crafts Projects for Children

Suggested Materials
Paper or plastic cups
Washable markers
Paper plates
Glue
Construction paper
Scissors
Crayons
Glitter or small decorative beads

Children can prepare for the Seder by making a Kiddush cup, a Seder plate, an Israeli flag, and a Mizrach.

The Kiddush Cup
By using paper or plastic cups, construction paper, glue, beads, glitter, markers and/or crayons children can design their own Kiddush cups for use at the Seder. You may encourage them to use some of the themes of the different cups like the Patriarchs, Matriarchs, Kings and Judges of Israel, or the great Zionist thinkers and activists.

The Seder Plate
The Seder plate should be large enough to contain seven small plates for the Seven Species of produce mentioned in the Torah, as well as small plates for carob, a root vegetable, a root vegetable with a tied scallion or leak leaf, an edible flower, edible seeds, and fruit from the land of Israel. Thirteen plates in total will be needed.

Ideally, the seven species of produce—wheat, barley, grapes, figs, pomegranates, olives, and dates—should be placed in the center of the plate. Then the other food items can be placed around the circumference of the seven species.

The Mizrach

A Mizrach is a picture hung on the eastern wall of a room to illustrate the direction of Jerusalem. During the Seder children will be asked to hang the Mizrach that they made. To make a Mizrach with a child first explain that you will be making a picture that will help remind people of the direction of the land of Israel. Then provide the children with all of the supplies listed on the previous page. They will need to either draw a picture or cut and paste a number of smaller pictures to make one bigger picture. The finished product will be hung on the eastern wall of the dining room where the Seder will be held.

Israeli Flag

An alternative to making a Mizrach is to ask the children to draw an Israeli flag. Using a large piece of construction paper and markers or crayons, the children can quickly draw their own Israeli flag. While they are making the flag, explain to them that their drawing will be an important part of the Seder, since it will be used to point out the direction of the land of Israel. After the children have made the flag ask them what the Israeli flag means to them. Tell them what the flag means to you.

Helpful Web Sites

Click on these sites for fun, interesting ideas to involve your children in an Israel Seder.

- **The Jewish Agency for Israel: http://www.jafi.org.il**
(Click on "Education and Identity," then "Jewish and Zionist Activities.")

- **The Israel Ministry of Foreign Affairs**
http://www.mfa.gov.il/mfa/mfaarchive/1900_1949

- **The Coalition for the Advancement of Jewish Education**
http://www.caje.org (click on the "Curriculum Bank")

APPENDIX L

Causing the Seeds of Israel's Future to Grow

Contact Form

Name:_____

Address:_____

Telephone Number:_____

I will not be silent and will not sit still while Israel's existence is being threatened. Instead, over the next month I will take a stand to protect the State of Israel and help it grow by offering my time to the following organization(s):

The program I will volunteer in
is:_____

I would like to help out by doing:_____

I will have time to volunteer on:

Monday   Tuesday   Wednesday   Thursday   Friday   Sunday

Please state times and circle:

From _____ A.M. P.M. TO_____ A.M. P.M.

APPENDIX M

Ways You Can Get Involved to Ensure Israel's Survival

AIPAC:
Support Legislation that Condemns Terrorism and Supports Israel
The American Israel Public Affairs Committee
444 Madison Avenue
22nd Floor
New York, NY 10022
Tel: 212-750-4110
Fax: 212-750-4125
Email: nyreg@aipac.org
Website: http://www.aipac.org

American Friends of Ben Gurion University
Support the Ongoing Development of an Educational and High-Tech "Hotspot" in the Negev Desert
Angie Lee Senior Associate Director
1430 Broadway
8th Floor
New York, NY 10018
Tel: 212-687-7721
Fax 212-302-6443
Email: info@aabgu.org
Website: www.aabgu.org

American Friends of Hebrew University
Support the Intellectual Capital of the Israeli Public
One Battery Park Plaza, 25th Floor
New York, NY 10004
Tel: (212) 607-8500, (800) 567-2348
Fax: (212) 809-4430
Email: info@afhu.org
Website: www.afhu..org

American Society of the University of Haifa
American Friends of Haifa University
Support the Efforts of a Small Israeli University to Help Maintain the City's Intellectual Capital in Order to Effectively Compete in the Global Economy.
Ms. Teri Normand Director
220 Fifth Avenue Suite 1301
New York, NY 10001
Tel: 1-212-685-7880
Fax: 1-212-685-7883
E-mail: tnormand@asuh.org
Website: http://www.asuh.org/
http://www.jcfphoenix.org/grants-jeworg.html

American Friends of Magen David Adom-
American Red Magen David for Israel:
"Support Israel's National Emergency Medical Ambulance and Blood Service Society."
888 Seventh Avenue
Suite 403
New York, NY 10106
Tel: 212-757-1627
Fax: 212-757-4662
E-mail:info@armdi.org
Website: www.armdi.org

This not-for-profit, tax-exempt organization, is the authorized organization in the U.S. to raise funds for Magen David Adom in Israel. Its Blood Center supplies 100% of the blood requirements for the Israel Defense Forces, 95% of the blood needs of Israel's hospitals and general population, and also conducts important cutting edge research in the field of hematology.

It supports Israeli Emergency Medical Assistance and Israeli Red Magen David Ambulances and supplies blood for Israel's Blood Disaster Services. Assistance to this organization benefits Israel's entire population.

Contributions are used for the following purposes:
To supply and equip ambulances. bloodmobiles, and cardiac rescue ambulances serving all hospitals and communities throughout Israel

To provide supplies and equipment for the Red Magen David blood bank and MDA Fractionation Institute

To provide scholarships and education funds to train paramedics, laboratory technicians, and scientists

Programs that offer support include the following:
Magen David Adom is in critical need of funding for its Blood Center as terrorism has placed a severe drain on its resources. Those wishing to help should contact Sybil Weingast at American Red Magen David for Israel at 212-757-1627 or email Info@armdi.org.

MDA Youth Volunteers Organization trains Israel's youth and non-Israeli volunteers who are interested in volunteering to work at the Magen David Adom Emergency Medical Stations throughout Israel; this volunteer program lasts several weeks. Those interested in volunteering should also contact Sybil Weingast at American Red Magen David for Israel at 212-757-1627 or email Info@armdi.org.

American Friends of Tel Aviv University
"Raise Funds for the Development and Advancement of Higher Education, Research and Training in all Branches of Knowledge in Israel and Elsewhere."
39 Broadway, 15th Floor
New York, NY 10006
Phone: 212-742-9070, 1-800-989-1198
Fax: 212-742-9071
E-Mail: info@tauac.org
Primary use of charitable funds are for University projects.

American Friends of the IDF
Support the Soldiers Who are Risking their Lives to Defend Israel
298 Fifth Ave.—5th Floor
New York, NY 10001
Tel: 212-244-3118
Fax: 212-244-3119
E-mail: fidf@israelsoldiers.org
Website: www.israelsoldiers.org/about.cfm

ARZA
Support Reform Judaism's Main Vehicle for Advocacy, and Zionist Education
Association of Reform Zionists of America
Rabbi Stanley M. Davids President
633 Third Avenue
New York, NY 10017
Tel: 212-650-4000
Fax 212-650-4289
Email: arza@urj.org
Website: http://www.arza.org/

"ARZA is the Zionist arm of the Reform Movement and an affiliate of the Union for Reform Judaism, serving 1.5 million Reform/Progressive Jews. ARZA is the vehicle for the mass participation of American Reform Jews, focusing on Israel, with an emphasis on advocacy and travel; and Zionist education in America. ARZA's initiative ISRAEL MATTERS: Our Commitment to Israel provides the foundation for programming and advocacy relating to the core mission."[97]

Some of the programs sponsored are:
Mission to Israel
Help with mailings
Become a local ARZA Representative and Speaker at your temple
Participate in a Bar/Bat Mitzvah twinning program

Hasbara Fellowships:
Help Educate and Advocate for Israel on University Campuses
63 West 38th St. Suite 1103
New York, NY 10018
Tel: 646-365-0030
Email: director@israelactivism.com
Website: www.israelactivism.com

The Hasbara Fellowship is a program by *Aish HaTorah*, which trains university students to advocate for Israel on their University campuses.

Hadassah, the Women's Zionist Organization of America
Support Education, Healthcare, Youth Institutions and Land Development in Israel
Jonathan Rulnick
50 West 58 Street
New York, NY 10019
Tel: 212-303-8061
Fax: 212-303-4524
Email: memberinfo@hadassah.org
Website: www.hadassah.org

Hadassah, the Women's Zionist Organization of America, is a volunteer women's organization which promotes the unity of the Jewish people and supports health care facilities, educational programs and youth institutions, as well as land development to meet the country's changing needs. Becoming a member of Hadassah is strongly encouraged and is a good first step toward participating in a program which can make a difference.

Help Hadassah to Make a Difference in Israel
Hadassah offers tangible ways to connect with Israel and Zionism through:
Hadassah Medical Organization
Hadassah College Jerusalem
Hadassah Career Counseling Institute
Hadassah's Youth Aliyah/Children At Risk programs, helping disadvantaged Israeli children
Young Judea clubs, camps, and Israel programs
Partnering with the Jewish National Fund
In the US, Hadassah's 300,000 members promote Zionism, social action and advocacy, volunteerism, Jewish education, health education, and connections with Israel. [98]

Hatzolah:
Support Jerusalem's Volunteer Ambulance Service
American Friends of Hatzolah Jerusalem
7 Pinewood Drive
Monsey N.Y. 10952
Tel: 845-300-3101
Email: hatzolah@hatzolah.org.il
Website: www.hatzolah.org.il/

Hatzolah Israel, formerly known as Hatzolah Jerusalem, is a volunteer, non-profit Emergency Medical Service (EMS) that assists the victims of terrorism and other medical emergencies throughout Israel. Charitable contributions support the purchase of medical life saving equipment as well as training volunteers in effectively responding to emergencies.

Hillel:
Support Israel on University Campuses Throughout the United States
Hillel: The Foundation for Jewish Campus Life
Charles and Lynn Schusterman International Center
Arthur and Rochelle Belfer Building
800 Eighth Street, NW
Washington, DC 20001-3724
Tel: 202-449-6500
Fax: 202-449-6600
Email: info@israeloncampuscoalition.org
Website: http://www.hillel.org

The university campus has become a breeding ground for anti-Israel protests that spread untruthful slanderous remarks about Israel. Hillel is the sole source of Israel advocacy and Jewish life on many university campuses throughout the United States. Programs offered by Hillel provide education and opportunities for students to advocate for Israel through programs like:

Israel on Campus Coalition
Birthright Israel
Hillel Pardes Summer Learning Institute
Israel advocacy Mission and Training Seminar
Student Leadership Mission to Israel[99]

Honenu:
Help Provide Legal Aid to Israeli Soldiers Prosecuted for Defending Themselves in an Emergency
POB # 2
Kiryat Arba 90100
Israel
Tel: 011-972-2-9605558
Tel: 972-0-2-9605558
Email: webmaster@ayalla.net
Website: www.honenu.org.il

Israel Bonds:
Help Support Israel's Economy During Times of Economic Crisis
State of Israel Bonds
New York Region
575 Lexington Avenue, 11th Floor
New York, NY 10022
Tel: 1-888-244-4808
1-800-229-9650
Fax: 212-644-7014
Email: newyork@israelbonds.com
Website: www.israelbonds.com

"Proceeds realized from the sale of Israel bonds and other securities are utilized by Israel's Finance Ministry to help fund projects in key economic sectors. Examples include:

Agriculture
Industry
Shipping
Energy
Transportation
Communications
Water resources
Immigrant absorption"[100]

Israeli Soldiers Missing in Action
Help Bring Back Israeli Soldiers who are Missing in Action
ICMIS
P.O. Box 32380
Jerusalem 91322
Israel
Tel: 011-972-2-623-6083
Fax: 011-972-2-623-3864
E-mail: info@mia.org.il
Website: www.mia.org.il/

Those who wish to help can:
Volunteer to organize events or programs in your own community, synagogue, school or youth group, with the purpose of raising awareness of this painful issue.

Participate in lobbying campaigns where you can write elected officials to help return soldiers or at least bring closure for families of missing soldiers.
Sign the 1,000,000 Voice Petition
Wear Dog Tags with the names of Missing Israeli Soldiers (can be purchased through the organization).
Make a Donation

Jewish Agency for Israel:
Help Ensure the Continuity of the Jewish People with a Strong Israel at its Core
2303 Cumberland Parkway
Suite 300
Atlanta, GA 30339
USA
Phone: 770-438-1441
Fax: 770-438-7841
Email: avramk@jafi-na.org
Website: http://www.jafi.org.il
Website for those who wish to Volunteer:
http://www.jafi.org.il/aliyah/english/article.aspx?id=410

The Jewish Agency supports programs for young people who want to help Israel and be a strong part of the Jewish community.
Volunteer opportunities include the following:
Office-based internships
Project *Areivem*, which connects Federations with their Israel
Partnership 2000 regions and their adoptive cities
Israel-based internships
Assisting in the absorption of new Israeli immigrants

Jewish Community Relations Council
Help Advocate Locally for Israel
PO Box 4176,
111 Kinderkamack Road
River Edge, NJ 07661
Ruth Siev
Tel: 201-488-6800
Fax: 201-457-0960
Website: www.ujannj.org

Israel Affairs Committee supports pro-Israel advocacy through letter writing campaigns, development of educational programs, and organization of leadership missions to Israel

Jewish National Fund:
Help Repair Israel's Forests from the Damage Done by Terrorism
JNF of Greater New York
42 East 69th Street
New York, NY 10021
Tel: 212-879-9300
Fax: 212-570-1673
Email: communications@jnf.org
Website: www.jnf.org

Volunteers can get involved by supporting JNF in their seven action areas:
Forestry and Ecology
Water
Community Development
Security
Education
Research and Development
Tourism and Recreation

MERCAZ USA
Support the Conservative Movement's Organization for Israel Advocacy, and Zionist Education
Mercaz
155 Fifth Avenue
New York, NY 10010
Tel: 212-533-7800 x 2016
Fax 212-533-2601
Email: info@mercazusa.org
Website: www.mercazusa.org

Take part in educational events, political lobbying, missions to Israel, and programs to support and assist Aliyah.

The American Committee for the Weizmann Institute of Science

Support Research which Focuses on the Most Vital Problems in Health and Medicine

The American Committee for the Weizmann Institute of Science Support basic science research focusing on the most vital problems in health, medicine, and technology.

Robert B. Machinist, Chairman
633 Third Avenue
New York, NY 10017
Tel: 212.895.7900
Fax: 212.895.7999
Email: info@acwis.org
Website: www.weizmann-usa.org

The Weizmann Institute is one of the world's foremost centers of interdisciplinary scientific research and graduate study. Its 2,500 scientists, students, technicians, and engineers pursue basic research in the quest for knowledge to enhance the quality of human life. New ways of fighting disease and hunger, protecting the environment, and harnessing alternative sources of energy are high priorities at Weizmann. Join them in their mission of Science for the Benefit of Humanity.

Charitable contributions can be made to:
Science for the Benefit of Humanity Fund
The President's Contingency Fund
Laboratory Monthly Partners Fund

The American Jewish Committee:

Advocate for Israel
Robert Goodkind President
165 East 56th Street
New York, NY 10022-2746
Tel: 212-751-4000
Fax: 212-891-1492
Email: PR@ajc.org
Website: www.ajc.org

The American Jewish Committee seeks to ensure Jewish continuity and deepen ties between America and Israel. They also seek to ensure that Jews around the world can live in safety. Their method for accomplishing this task is by seeking to promote a stronger more pluralistic world.

Volunteers can become involved in the following programs:
AJC Fellows program
Hands Across the Campus
Catholic/Jewish Educational Enrichment Program
Leadership Training Program

The North American Conference on Ethiopian Jewry:
Help the Ethiopian Jewish Community in Israel Integrate into Israeli Society
132 Nassau Street
Suite 412
New York, NY 10038
Tel: 212-233-5200
Email: nacoej@aol.com
Website: www.nacoej.org

"The North American Conference on Ethiopian Jewry (NACOEJ) is a grass-roots, non-profit organization founded in 1982 with four mandates:
To help Ethiopian Jews survive in Ethiopia.
To assist them in reaching Israel.
To aid in their absorption into Israeli society.
To preserve their unique and ancient culture."[101]

Assistance is needed in all of the following programs:
For Americans who wish to help Ethiopian Jews in Israel
Adopt a High School Student
Adopt a College Student
Provide School Supplies
Bar/Bat Mitzvah Twinning
For Americans who wish to help Ethiopian Jews who are still in Ethiopia
Support Embroidery Program
Lunch Sponsorship Program

The One Family Fund:
Provide Assistance to Victims of Terrorism
Sari Singer, East Coast Director
Sharon Feingold, Administrator
494 Broad Street
Newark, NJ 07102
Tel: 973-438-3535
Toll-Free 1-866-9-1FAMILY
1-866-913-2645
Fax: 973.438.1399
Volunteers should contact Yehuda Poch at:
Email: info@onefamilyfund.org
Website: www.onefamilyfund.org
One Family is the central organization in Israel providing assistance to victims of terrorism. It helps over 2,200 victims of terror and their families on a daily basis.
Volunteers can become involved through participating in the following:
Adopt-a-Family program
Bar/Bat Mitzvah Twinning programs
Hosting Victim's Missions to Your Community: These missions provide further education and increase support for Israeli victims of terror

The One Family Fund is also in need of volunteer coordinators in communities throughout the world to assist in publicizing events and raising funds for much-needed programs. Volunteer coordinators are also needed to work with schools, synagogues, youth groups, and other community organizations so they can become involved in helping Israeli victims of terror.

Tmura—The Israeli Public Service Venture Fund
Support the Development of Israeli Non-Profits Through a Venture Capital Investment
C/o Gross Kleinhendler,
1 Azrieli Center
Tel Aviv, 67021 ISRAEL
Tel: 011-972-3-607-4506
Fax: 011-972-3-691-4164
Email: info@tmura.org
Website: www.tmura.org

Tmura—The Israeli Public Service Venture Fund is a nonprofit organization which was established in 2002 by the Israeli venture capital and high-tech communities. Promoting a new model for philanthropy and a new standard for investments, Tmura is creating a culture of giving within the high-tech sector by enabling companies to donate equity to support education and youth-related initiatives in Israel. We invite you to partner with us in this effort—help us increase the "size of the pie" and inculcate a culture of giving within the high-tech community, a sector that can have a tremendous impact on the philanthropic landscape in Israel.

Vacation in Israel
Fly to Israel with El Al
15 E. 26th St. 6th floor
New York, U.S.A.
Tel: 212-768-9200
1-800- 223-6700
Fax: 212-852-0641
E-Mail: addresbook@elalusa.com
Website: http://www.elal.co.il

El Al Sponsors the Following Tours
Classical Tour
Bibleland Tour
Kibbutz Experience
Last Moment Package

**Visit the Following Websites to Shop in Israel
while Staying in America**
www.shopinisrael.com
www.israelexport.org
http://www.ou.org/israel/5762/supporteconomy.htm
http://www.israeliproducts.com
http://www.israeliproducts.com/2ndlevelpages/services.html
http://www.ahavat-israel.com/ahavat/am/charity.asp

Yad Sarah:
Help Israel's Elderly
450 Park Avenue, Suite 3201
New York, New York 10022
Tel. 212-223-7758
Fax: 212-223-7759
Toll Free: 1-866-YAD-SARAH
E-mail: yadsarahny@earthlink.net
Website: http://www.yadsarah.org/

This organization benefits Israel's elderly and is dependent solely on private contributions. Volunteers are needed to contribute both their time and their finances to support core programs. Yad Sarah lends medical equipment to elderly, runs a geriatric dentistry clinic, and provides legal services for the elderly. Volunteers are needed to assist Yad Sarah in gaining greater exposure to the American and worldwide Jewish Community.

World Zionist Organization
Emily Sigalow
New York Regional Director
New York - United States of America
Tel: 212-339-6922
Fax: 212-318-6127
Email: emilys@hagshama.org.il
Website: www.wzo.org.il/en/default.asp

The Hagshama Department encourages young people to begin a journey towards self discovery and empowerment. Programs are designed to instill in each participant a sense of belonging and responsibility to the broader community. The process of growth is seen as beginning with one's self and expanding to develop a deep commitment and responsibility for the Jewish community at large and eventually to the State of Israel.

The Following Programs are Offered:
Kibbutz Volunteer
Volunteers for Israel (3-Week Volunteer Program in the Israeli Army)
Ulpan Conversational Hebrew Courses
Professional Internships
Yeshiva Study

Zionist Organization of America
Support the Oldest, and One of the Largest, Pro-Israel Organizations in America.
4 East 34th Street
New York, NY 10016
Tel: 212-481-1500
Fax: 212-481-1515
Email: info@zoa.org
Website: www.zoa.org

The World Zionist Organization provides educational opportunities to learn more about Israel and Zionism with the purpose of increasing Israel advocacy in America and around the world.

ENDNOTES

1. *Pentateuch and Haftorah*, Deuteronomy 30: 5. New York, NY: Soncino Press, (1960).
2. *Pentateuch and Haftorah*, Exodus 16: 15.
3. *The Judaic Classics: Complete Tanach with Rashi: Complete Tanach with Rashi CD ROM*, Chicago IL: Judaica Press/Davka Corporation, (1999). Hereafter cited as *The Judaic Classics: Complete Tanach with Rashi*. Exodus 40: 22-23 also see Chronicles I, 23: 28-30.
4. *Siddur Ahavas Shalom: The Complete Artscroll Siddur*, Artscroll Mesorah Series pp. 721 Brooklyn, NY: Mesorah Publications Ltd, 1984, pp. 721.
5. Ibid.
6. *The Pentateuch and Haftorah*, Genesis 13: 15.
7. *The Pentateuch and Haftorah*, Deuteronomy 8: 8.
8. Reich, Bernard Reich. "Chronology of Major Jewish Events," *Israel: Land Tradition and Conflict*. Boulder, CO: Westview Press, 1985, "Chronology of Major Jewish Events" pp. 199-202.
9. *The Judaic Classics Classics: Complete Tanach with Rashi CD ROM*, Samuel, 11:15.
10. Reich, Bernard. pp. 199-202.
11. Ibid.
12. *The Judaic Classics Classics: Complete Tanach with Rashi CD ROM*, Kings, 23: 24.
13. Reich, Bernard. pp. 199-202.
14. Ibid.
15. Ibid.
16. Solomon Grayzel, Solomon, *A History of the Jews*. New York, NY: Penguin, 1984, pp. 176-77.
17. Ibid, p. 176.
18. Dan Bahat, ed., *Twenty Centuries of Jewish Life in the Holy Land*, Jerusalem, Israel: The Israel Economist: 1976. Quoted in Mitchell Bard, (2001) *Myths and Facts: A Guide to the Arab Israeli Conflict*. American Israeli Cooperative Enterprise, Chevy Chase, MD: 2001.
19. *The Judaic Classics Classics: Complete Tanach with Rashi CD ROM*, Leviticus 26:38.
20. *The Judaic Classics Classics: Complete Tanach with Rashi CD ROM*, Deuteronomy 28:32.
21. Lewis, Bernard Lewis. *The Jews of Islam*, Princeton, NJ: Princeton University Press. 1984, pp. 158.
22. Roumani, Maurice. *(1977). The Case of Jews in Arab Countries: A Neglected Issue*, Tel Aviv, Israel: Tel Aviv World Organization of Jews from Arab Countries, 1977, pp. 26-27. Quoted in Mitchell Bard, *Myths and Facts: A Guide to the Arab Israeli Conflict*, American Israeli Cooperative Enterprise, Chevy Chase MD: American Israeli Cooperative Enterprise, 2001. See also Bat Yeor, *The Dhimmi*, Teaneck, NJ: Farleigh Dickinson University Press, 1985.
23. P.E. Grosser, P.E., & E.G. Halperin, E.G. *"Anti-Semitism: Causes and Effects,"* New York, NY: Philosophic Library, 1978.
24. Ibid.
25. Ibid. Grayzel, Solomon, pp. 362.
26. Grosser, P.E., & Halperin, E.G.
27. Twain, Mark. *Innocents Abroad*. New York, NY: The New American Library, (1881).

28. Reich, Bernard. *Israel: Land Tradition and Conflict*, pp. 52.
29. *The Babylonian Talmud: Sefer Taaniyot Eilu*, 3: 29-30, New York, NY: Soncino Press: 1990.
30. Grosser , P.E., & Halperin, E.G.
31. R. Lippman, R., "Gates to Jewish Heritage," website: The Holocaust, http://www. jewishgates.com, 2004. See also Grayzel, pp. 662-663.
32. Reich, Bernard. pp. 58. See also Grayzel, pp. 678.
33. "The State of Israel.com" website http://www.stateofisrael.com/ anthem/, on November 2004.
34. *The Judaic Classics Classics: Complete Tanach with Rashi*, Psalms 121:4.
35. Ibid, Isaiah 43:5-6.
36. Ibid, Isaiah 27:13.
37. Ibid, Isaiah 35:2.
38. Ibid, Isaiah 51:3.
39. *The Babylonian Talmud: Sefer Kiddushin*, New York, NY: Soncino Press, 1990, 49 p. b.
40. *The Judaic Classics Classics: Complete Tanach with Rashi*, Psalm 128: 5.
41. The Orthodox Union, "The Prayer for the Israel Defense Forces," http://www.ou.org /forms/tehillim.htm. New York, NY: The Orthodox Union, 2003.
42. Soncino Press: *The Babylonian Talmud: Sefer Bava Batra*, New York, NY: Soncino Press: 1990, 8 p. b.
43. D. Olivestone, D. Editor and Translator. *NCSY Bencher: A Book of Prayer and Song*, Rochester, NY: The Union Of Orthodox Jewish Congregations of America, 1982.
44. *The Judaic Classics Classics: Complete Tanach with Rashi*: Isaiah 62:1.
45. *Pentateuch and Haftorah*, Genesis 13:14. New York, NY: Soncino Press, 1960.
46. Ibid, Genesis 32:27.
47. Reich, Bernard. p.p. 199-202.
48. *Pentateuch and Haftorah*, Deuteronomy 34: 1.
49. *The Judaic Classics Classics: Complete Tanach with Rashi*, Joshua 3: 1-17.
50. Ibid, Deuteronomy 8:8.
51. Reich, Bernard. pp. 199-202.
52. *The Judaic Classics Classics: Complete Tanach with Rashi* Judges 16:29.
53. Reich, Bernard. pp. 199-202.
54. *The Judaic Classics Classics: Complete Tanach with Rashi*: Judges 4:1-24.
55. Ibid. Samuel Book I, 11: 14-15.
56. Ibid. Samuel Book 2, 2:4.
57. Ibid. Kings Book I, 6:1.
58. Reich, Bernard. 1985 pp. 199-202.
59. Grayzel, Solomon, pp. 34-46.
60. Ibid. pp. 61-70.
61. Ibid. pp. 174-178.
62 Ibid. pp. 165-167.
63. Ibid. pp. 175-177.
64. Rav Sig: Rabbinic Genealogy Special Interest Group, www.jewishgen.org/ rabbinic/infofiles/rabbis.htm Retrieved March 11th 2004. See also The Jewish Agency for Israel, "A Timeline of Jewish Historical Events." Jerusalem, Israel, reprinted on the website http://ww.jewishhistory.org.il/ Nov. 2004
65. Adapted from The International Coalition for Missing Israeli Soldiers, http://www.mia.org.il/prayer/index.html, October, 2004.

66. Azzam Pasha, Secretary General of the Arab League, May 15 1948, reprinted in Mitchell Bard, *Myths and Facts: A Guide to the Arab Israeli Conflict*, Chevy Chase, MD: American Israeli Cooperative Enterprise, 2001.
67. Dr. Jarerr Al-Kidwah, advisor to Yassir Arafat, aired on Palestinian Authority TV (Yassir Arafat controlled) 11/29/01, reprinted in Bard.
68. Sermon of Sheikh Ibrahim Mahdi a few days after Yasser Arafat's cease fire declaration. Aired on Palestinian Authority Television (Yassir Arafat controlled) June 8, 2001. Reprinted in Bard.
69. Bard, pp. 346–353.
70. Yael Zisling, "A Brief Chronology of Wine Making in Israel." *http://www.gems_in_Israel.com/e_article000033150.htm*, August– September 2001. George Medovoy, "Israel's Wine Awakening: Where Antiquity Merges with the Present." Published by Yael Zisling, *http://www.gemsinIsrael.com/e_article 000033152.htm*, Adar, 2002. *Daniel Rogov, Daniel Rogov's Guide to Israeli Wines*, New Milford, CT:Toby Press, 2004
71. Barbara Weill, from *Lexicon of Zionism*, expanded and updated by Dr. Judy Rosen, and edited by Gila Ansell Brauner., posted on the Jewish Agency for Israel Website http://www.jafi.org.il/education/100/gloss/index.html.
72. Theodor Herzl, "Address to First Zionist Congress," Basel Switzerland, 1897; reprinted in Arthur Hertzberg, *The Zionist Idea*, New York, NY: The Jewish Publication Society of America,1959.
73. Rabbi Abraham Isaac Kook, "The Land of Israel 1910–1930" Orot 1942, reprinted in Hertzberg.
74. Rabbi Meir Bar Ilan, "What kind of Life in Eretz Israel?," 1922, reprinted in Hertzberg.
75. Rabbi Samuel Mohilever, "Message to the First Zionist Congress," 1897, reprinted in Hertzberg.
76. Rabbi Yehudah Alkalai, "The Third Redemption," 1843, reprinted in Hertzberg.
77. Solomon Schecter, "Zionism: A Statement," 1906, reprinted in Hertzberg.
78. Kol HaTor, 1:5, reprinted on the "Israel Ministry of Foreign Affairs" website, http://www.mfa.gov.il, November 1, 2004.
79. Yehiel Michael Pines, "Jewish Nationalism Cannot be Secular," 1906. p. 189. Reprinted in Hertzberg,
80. Ahad Ha Am, "The Law of the Heart," 1894, reprinted in Hertzberg.
81. Chaim Nachman Bialik "Address at the Inauguration of the Hebrew University of Jerusalem," January 4, 1925. reprinted in Hertzberg.
82. Chaim Weitzmann, "Reminiscences," 1927, reprinted in Hertzberg.
83. Martin Buber, "Hebrew Humanism," 1942–1927, reprinted in Hertzberg.
84. Leo Pinsker, "Auto Emancipation," 1882. 1942–1927, reprinted in Hertzberg.
85. Judah Leon Magnes, "Like all Nations," 1930, reprinted in Hertzberg.
86. Ibid.
87. Louis Dembitz Brandies, "The Jewish Problem and How to Solve It." 1915, reprinted in Hertzberg.
88. David Ben Gurion, excerpts from a speech entitled 'The Imperatives of The Jewish Revolution," 1944, reprinted in Hertzberg.
89. Golda Meir, "Address to the Knesset" Tel Aviv, Israel: 26 May 1970, reprinted on the "Gift of Speeches" website http://gos.sbc.edu/m/meir.html, November 2004.
90. Max Nordau, "Zionism", 1902, reprinted in Hertzberg.

91. Theodor Herzl, "The Jewish State", 1896, reprinted in Hertzberg.
92. Vladimir Jabotinsky, "The Ideology of Betar" January 21, 1929, reprinted on the "World Zionist Organization" website, under "Essential Zionist Texts", http://www.wzo.org.il/en/resources/view.asp?id=116.
93. Ibid.
94. David Aaron Gordon, "Our Tasks Ahead", 1920, reprinted in Hertzberg.
95. Hannah Senesh, February 4, 1942, posted on the Jewish Agency for Israel website, http://www.jafi.org.il/education/moriya/caesarea/hanna.html, November 2004.
96. Henrietta Szold, "Zionism: The Cry of the Children in Palestine," Speech Addressing the Vaad Leumi of Jerusalem, September 13, 1936, posted on the "The World Zionist Organization" website http://www.wzo.org.il/en/resources/view.asp?id= 1622&subject=28, November 2004.
97. "Association of Reform Zionists of America (ARZA)" website, http://www.arza.org/index.cfm?id=270 November 2004.
98. "Hadassah The Women's Zionist Organization of America" website, http://www.hadassah.org/pageframe.asp?section=about&page=whoweare.html&header=whoweare&size=50. November 2004.
99. "Hillel: The Foundation for Jewish Campus Life" website, http://www.hillel.org/Hillel/NewHille.nsf/index. November 2004.
100. "Israel Bonds" website, http://www.israelbonds.com/aboutus.html. November 2004.
101. "The North American Conference on Ethioian Jewry" website, http://www.nacoej.org/mission.htm. November 2004.